Sunday Mass Five Years from Now

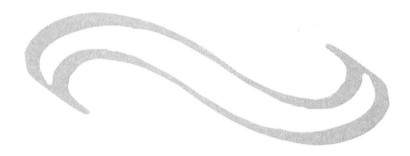

Gabe Huck

LITURGY
TRAINING
PUBLICATIONS

SUNDAY MASS FIVE YEARS FROM NOW © 2001 Archdiocese
of Chicago: Liturgy Training Publications, 1800 North
Hermitage Avenue, Chicago IL 60622-1101; 1-800-933-1800;
fax 1-800-933-7094; orders@ltp.org. All rights reserved.

Visit our website at www.ltp.org.

Thanks to Kathy Luty for reviewing, editing and adding
resources throughout the manuscript. This book was edited
by David Philippart and designed by Lucy Smith. Bryan Cones
was the production editor, and Karen Mitchell was the production artist. The typefaces are Optima, Times Italic and
Voluta Script. *Sunday Mass Five Years from Now* was printed
in Canada by Webcom Limited.

05 04 03 02 01   5 4 3 2 1

Library of Congress Cataloging-in-Publication Data

Huck, Gabe.
    Sunday Mass five years from now/Gabe Huck.
        p. cm.
    ISBN 1-56854-188-0
  1. Mass. 2. Vatican Council (2nd : 1962–1965) I. Title.
    BX2215.3 .H83 2001
    264'.02036—dc21

2001029609

FIVE

Contents

∾

Before Year One   1

An Invitation

Resources to Gather for Year One   15

Year One   16
Prepare the Leaders to Lead

Resources to Gather for Year Two   30

Year Two   31
The Communion Rite

Resources to Gather for Year Three   68

Year Three   69
The Eucharistic Prayer

Resources to Gather for Year Four   93

Year Four   94
The Liturgy of the Word

Resources to Gather for Year Five   121

Year Five   122
Entrance and Concluding Rites

Now What Do We Do?   145

Before Year One
An Invitation

In the fourth decade of the liturgical renewal mandated by the Second Vatican Council (1962–65), I want to make some practical suggestions to parishes about their Sunday liturgy. This comes from two convictions. First, many parishes have worked hard to implement well the reforms of the Council. Second, with few exceptions, parishes have stopped far short of what is needed and mandated.

To my knowledge, the best visions of what is needed and mandated are found in the pastoral letters of two American bishops: *Our Communion, Our Peace, Our Promise* (1984), addressed to the church of Chicago by Cardinal Joseph Bernardin, and *Gather Faithfully Together* (1997), addressed to the church of Los Angeles by Cardinal Roger Mahony. The Sunday liturgy they urge in these letters is characterized by that "full, conscious and active" participation that is at the core of the *Constitution on the Sacred Liturgy.* That is so because these two bishops write of the *habit* of Sunday liturgy, the longed-for deeds of an assembly—presider, ministers and all the faithful— gathering each Lord's Day to do what is their baptismal right and duty. This book takes the vision of these two pastoral letters as a parish goal and asks: How do we get there? Like the New York cab driver's answer to "Can you tell me how to get to Carnegie Hall?" our answer is "Practice, practice, practice!"

"Practice!" The cab driver's imperative verb is not merely doing the same thing over and over again. Used as a verb, practice means doing the same thing over and over anew. As a noun, practice means how something is done, almost a synonym for "way," as in, "The Catholic practice is to anoint the sick with oil, to feed the hungry, to act responsibly toward creation." And practice, verb or noun, is a way we speak respectfully of some professions: "She practices medicine."

This is a book about our practice of liturgy in all three of these meanings. First, practice is about respect for what the liturgy is, and liturgy is ritual, something we do over and over, over and over *by heart,* over and over *anew.* Second, practice requires recognizing how Catholic liturgy and Catholic life constitute a single practice, a way of living that has taken on all sorts of local expressions as it attempts to embody the gospel. Our liturgical practice and our day-to-day practice as baptized people are not so much linked as they are different sides of the same coin. Third, practice is the discipline that is our vocation. If the lawyer practices law, and the doctor practices medicine, the Catholic practices the paschal mystery of our Lord Jesus Christ, who has died, is risen and will come again. That is the meaning and content of both our liturgy and our life.

How do we get there? How do we get to where Cardinals Bernardin and Mahony, along with many others, have imagined? Practice. This is a book about parish practicing. It is a unique approach, and it stands on these principles:

- *Even a parish that has done much already will need time, so take time and do it well.*

- *Don't take "five years" literally.*

- *Get everybody on board first.*

- *Work on one thing at a time.*

Can We Agree on This?

The Council's teaching in the *Constitution on the Sacred Liturgy* is either wrong (we tried it and it didn't work) or is still untested. The challenge was and is immense. Before Vatican II, the ritual books of the church were minute descriptions of how the ordained person performed the rite. There was generally no acknowledgment that an assembly might be present. It wasn't important, except in theory.

Immediately after Vatican II, following its directives, the church began to renew its ritual books, fumbling toward the understanding of liturgy embraced by the Council. But who had any experience with this? No Catholic then alive had lived in a church that looked at liturgy the way the Council said we must look at liturgy. To make things even more difficult, the qualities that the Council made essential to the renewal of the liturgy were qualities that in the world of Western values were becoming less and less important: participation and community, to name two.

Indeed, it is a great wonder that the Council fathers said what they did! Even more, it is a great wonder that after more than three decades of effort, we haven't given up on trying to find and live that life. Some have, of course, and one can understand why.

The mandates of the *Constitution on the Sacred Liturgy* and the documents that attempted to begin its implementation, must, according to the words of the liturgy constitution itself, begin and end in article 14, where the task of the renewal is defined, the standard of success boldly set down:

> *The Church earnestly desires that all the faithful be led to that full, conscious, and active participation in liturgical celebrations called for by the very nature of the liturgy. Such participation by the Christian people as "a chosen race, a royal priesthood, a holy nation, God's own people" (1 Peter 2:9; see 2:4–5) is their right and duty by reason of their baptism.*

In the reform and promotion of the liturgy, this full and active participation by all the people is the aim to be considered before all else. For it is the primary and indispensable source from which the faithful are to derive the true Christian spirit and therefore pastors must zealously strive in all their pastoral work to achieve such participation by means of the necessary instruction.

Yet it would be futile to entertain any hopes of realizing this unless, in the first place, the pastors themselves become thoroughly imbued with the spirit and power of the liturgy and make themselves its teachers. A prime need, therefore, is that attention be directed, first of all, to the liturgical formation of the clergy.

There we have it: no more audience, no more passivity. The liturgy will be liturgy when all the faithful participate fully, consciously, actively. The Council gave two fairly amazing reasons for this. The first has to do with the nature of the liturgy itself. If liturgy is a time when somebody does something and somebody else watches, it may be entertainment, but it's not liturgy. If liturgy is a time when somebody does something for somebody else, it may be an inspirational event, but it's not liturgy. If liturgy is a time when each individual is free to pursue his or her thoughts, prayers or plans, there may be a room full of Catholics, but they're not doing Catholic liturgy.

Liturgy is done by all. That is its nature. It is communal ritual. This has been hard for us to grasp because so much in our culture tells us that when people gather, they expect to get something—a good show, at least. They expect to be satisfied consumers of some bit of entertainment or therapy or inspiration. They do not expect to do anything. But if we want liturgy, we have no choice. It's to be done fully, consciously, actively by all, or it's something else, something other than liturgy.

The second reason that liturgy will be liturgy only when all the faithful participate fully, consciously and actively has to do with the nature of the church. Baptized people have a right and a duty (note how "right" and "duty" are used in the text quoted above), and the right and the duty are the same. Baptized people have a right to a liturgy in which they participate fully, consciously, actively. And baptized people also have a duty, an obligation, a responsibility to so participate. In speaking of baptism this way, the Council fathers ended centuries of looking at baptism as a mere cleansing from original sin. Instead, the liturgy constitution recognizes baptism as the entry into life in the church, when we who are baptized put on the Lord Jesus Christ, whose liturgy of praise and thanksgiving, of intercession and of lament, we are to share forever—as our right and our duty.

However much we study the history of the liturgy and the various sciences that have an impact on the liturgy and the arts through which the liturgy is celebrated, we must return again and again to the goal of full, conscious and active participation by all the baptized. The Council said it clearly: This kind of participation is the goal to be sought above all in the renewal of the liturgy. Even more, the Council explained why. And the reason, even all these years later, should move us to embrace the long effort at renewal with fresh eagerness.

Why work for a day when the assembly, Sunday by Sunday, will gather to do its work, to make its prayer, to process into and through and out of its liturgy? Why work for a day when to be deprived of one's assembly on a Sunday will be a genuine moment of longing and hunger? Why work for a day when we leave the assembly on Sunday not so much inspired or feeling better or smarter or holier but instead exhausted because of the way we have poured ourselves into "the work of the people," which is the meaning of "liturgy"?

Because, says Vatican II, when you have liturgy, when *all* the baptized are deeply engaged in their ritual of word and table, of intercession and praise, of thanksgiving and of communion, then you have the indispensable source of the true Christian spirit. You have made Catholics. You have made, little by little, Sunday by Sunday, people whose lives are taking on the shape of these Sunday deeds. It is not simply that the intercession and praise are echoed in the prayers of the household, but that those who intercede and those who praise are the world God loves, and this world is here being fashioned into a gospel world.

We must imagine our parish's Sunday liturgy some time in the future: The members of that assembly have come to know in their muscles and their bones, in their heart and soul, the rhythms and movements, the sounds and gestures and postures, the flow and the order, the ins and outs, the highs and the lows, the louds and quiets of what they do as church on Sunday. "Do" is of course crucial to that notion. The Sunday liturgy can be a *deed* so loved and so needed by the baptized of this parish, so longed for, so identifying, so strengthening, that not doing it is inconceivable.

Can we agree on that much?

Can we agree further that some of our notions of "good" liturgy have confused the interesting, the entertaining and the inspiring with the truly participatory? In doing so, we may have thought that the renewal of the liturgy would be accomplished by priests and musicians and others who engaged the assembly, sometimes more, sometimes less. But the key is participation in the liturgy by the whole church, not an engaging person or engaging talk or engaging music.

Can we agree further that some of our notions of "good" liturgy have confused the esthetically beautiful and the rhetorically powerful with the truly participatory? In doing so, we may have thought that the renewal of the liturgy (or the restoration of the liturgy, some would say) would be accomplished by rebuilding what is imagined now as a golden and universal pre–Vatican II piety built around a sincere but terribly literal understanding of Catholic sacrament. But again, the key is participation in the liturgy of the church, not a re-creation of the participation-starved and (only occasionally) esthetically pleasing rites of the Council of Trent.

If we agree on these major understandings, then we agree that the task set forth by the Council has been elusive but remains worth embracing in any parish.

Who Is Needed?

Two things need to be said about the intended users of this little manual. First, this book is intended for those who are not new in their dedication to preparing the liturgy for the people and the people for the liturgy. Those who have not given parish liturgy much attention already will not be interested in what is said here. But among those who have, I believe, there are many who realize that they have accomplished much and yet still have not crossed some barrier to full participation. The liturgy and especially the music have a priority in the parish; the ministers—including presiders and homilists—take their tasks seriously. The assembly is attentive and sings well—but that's it. If you asked 25 regular Mass-goers how they prepare for and how they take part in the eucharistic prayer, you'd get 20 blank stares. Even though people have been prepared, something more is desperately needed. But there's a cultural leap that hasn't been made and perhaps also a theological one. This won't be made simply by talking about it and agreeing. It will be made when leadership approaches the liturgy for what it is: the ritual that is done by all present. This book is nothing more than an exploration of how to do that.

You know that you already have at your disposal an abundance of resources for the renewal of the parish liturgy. What is offered here does not replace these (in fact as said above, it presumes that the parish is making ample use of the pastoral letters of Cardinals Bernardin and Mahony). This is rather a plan that flows from years of observing our successes and failures at doing what Vatican II mandated. This is a modest effort to be the missing piece, a way to get from here to there. This book is here today, gone tomorrow (or a few years from tomorrow), whereas other resources remain.

A second thing that needs to be said about this book and the task it suggests is this: Without strong leadership, liturgical renewal does not happen. That leadership must include the pastor and any other staff members (musician, liturgy director) whose primary responsibilities relate to the liturgy. But it must also include commitment and support from the entire staff. The staff, large or small, must recognize what it is getting into with a commitment to build a parish that lives from its liturgy so that the rest of the parish's work can continue and not be stalled because of the energy going into the liturgy. The staff must acknowledge the great size of the task ahead so that there is a commitment on the part of each staff member to discover in what way Sunday liturgy is vital to the school, to youth ministry, to the religious education program, to the tasks of outreach and to the day-to-day work of the parish management and finances—in short, to every part of parish life that has a place at the staff meeting table.

The experiences of parishes that have shown this kind of commitment to the liturgical renewal of Vatican II demonstrate that strong leadership is required. How it is exercised may vary, but what is clear to all is that pastor and staff have set an important direction, committed themselves fully to it, have painstakingly worked with all involved on direction and details, will deal kindly and patiently with those who express doubt or even anger, and will do their homework and be accountable to the assembly for this exercise of authority.

The need for leadership was understood from the day the *Constitution on the Sacred Liturgy* was ratified by Vatican II. Amazingly, it was a caution that the bishops wrote right into article 14, connecting it (even in the same sentence!) to what has been quoted above about full and active participation by all being the primary and indispensable source from which the faithful are to derive their true Christian spirit. That same sentence continues, "[T]herefore pastors must zealously strive in all their pastoral work to achieve such participation by means of the necessary instruction." The next sentence reveals the bishops' amazing insight into the process of the reform: "Yet it would be futile to entertain any hopes of realizing this unless, in the first place, the pastors themselves become thoroughly imbued with the spirit and power of the liturgy and make themselves its teachers."

The bishops were correct. To be "imbued with the spirit and power of the liturgy" must mean to live from the liturgy, to hunger and thirst for it and to draw one's nourishment from all its expressions. But the bishops of Vatican II did not know how to "imbue" pastors with the spirit and power of the liturgy. A few pastors were filled with its spirit; most were not—never having had an opportunity to experience such liturgy. And without pastors imbued with the liturgy's spirit, the goal to be sought above all others—active participation by all—has not been realized (exactly what the Council fathers predicted). Changes have been made, like the use of the vernacular. Scripture has been opened up. Ministers have taken their place in the liturgy. Homilies have improved. Spaces have been (if only slightly) reordered. And in many places, these changes have accomplished great good.

At the same time and in the same places, the mistaken directions mentioned earlier—"liturgy as entertainment" and "liturgy as esthetic experience" and (a carryover from before Vatican II) "liturgy as doing things in the right order"—all continue to thrive. Each misses the point of Vatican II; each abandons participation for something else entirely; each in fact prevents the celebration of liturgy and thus prevents pastors and assemblies from being imbued with the liturgy's spirit and power.

If we heed the Council's words about the pastors themselves becoming thoroughly imbued with the spirit and power of the liturgy, where might we go? The suggestion of this book is that in "pastors" we include the entire parish leadership with the actual pastor, and by "imbued" we mean a path toward understanding and experiencing the way that participation in the liturgical assembly of the church can order our Christian lives. This is not only the Sunday Mass but the whole complex of rites that can constitute Catholic practice.

Five Whole Years?

The "five years" in the title of this book is not to be taken literally—neither the "five" nor the "years." But it just may happen that both work for you. The "five years" really means several things.

First, "five years" means "five phases," which is how the units of this book are laid out: preparation phase, communion rite, eucharistic prayer, liturgy of the word, entrance and concluding rites. There could have been four or six or even ten if we divided the liturgy differently or if we went beyond Sunday Mass, but this book focuses only on Sunday Mass, and five seems to work well.

These five phases need not be the same length. In some areas the parish may have already done a good deal and only several months of attention will be needed. Other areas may require more than a year before things are done in the participatory manner we seek.

Second, "five years" suggests that even those who have worked hard still need time to achieve that fullness of participation in the liturgy that is called for in the *Constitution on the Sacred Liturgy.* Even though a whole generation has passed since Vatican II, many still think that the changes in the liturgy were implemented without preparation, without instruction, without understanding. There is no response to good catechesis about the liturgy more common than this: "Why didn't anyone ever tell me that?"

Perhaps there was no other way to implement the renewal at the time. But now we can learn from this. While participatory liturgy is never an automatic result of lengthy catechesis, neither is it possible apart from catechesis. Wisdom and time are needed to ruminate on the words and gestures and sounds of the liturgy, to ponder the implications, to learn a little history, to discover and share and reflect upon the our best experiences of ritual and prayer.

The nature of this project also requires time. Participatory liturgy isn't fostered when an assembly is simply told, "Beginning next week, stand—as the rubrics have taught for 30 years—during the communion procession." Nor does catechesis in the homily and bulletin about this important change over a period of weeks make for good liturgy. Beyond mere information, time is needed to learn to do something well, to get the experience into the body, the individual and the church, to be at home with it, to do it by heart. When we seek *participation* and not obedience, time is needed not only in the preparation but in the good implementation of what is to be done. That is why "years" may not be so far-fetched in thinking about this project.

Third, "five years" suggests that the process has an end. It is finite. We will eventually get where we want to be. The liturgy will always need attention, but it may not always require such concentrated effort. In fact, the practice that takes hold during these "five years" will itself transform the content of liturgy preparation. You will reach a place where the assembly is doing the liturgy of Vatican II and where the parish is living from this liturgy.

In many dioceses, parishes may wonder if anything that lasts longer than the current leadership is worth beginning. Five years may see a change of pastor or of other personnel. Such change could not only jeopardize the work that remains but undo what has been done. Many parishes have had this experience, and it is a concern. The only response is that we have no choice once we believe that what Vatican II mandated can and must be done, and that it is larger than all of our individual agendas, talents and faults.

Using This Book: The Plan

This book is a plan for going from where you are now to where we all ought to be. It suggests that this must begin with a commitment from and study by the parish leadership. Only when this is accomplished can the parish be called, in catechesis and preaching and other ways, to begin focusing on individual rites within the Sunday Mass, working gradually at each until that full, conscious and active participation in the ritual is the "by heart" deed of each Sunday assembly.

Read this short book through before making any plans at all. Consider whether it offers the help you need to make a blueprint for the renewal of parish liturgy. How might you explain to others the goal and the process? In this first reading, and later in the detailed work, mark up these wide margins with your own thoughts, concerns and questions, and with notes on group discussions.

The premise for this plan is simple: If we take the basic moments of Sunday liturgy one at a time and devote adequate time to study, catechesis and implementation of that rite according to the standards of the liturgy constitution, we will make a parish order of Sunday liturgy that can and will be strong enough to sustain the Sunday-by-Sunday repetition. We will make a liturgy in which it is self-evident that the norm is the full and conscious and active participation of all the baptized, who in fact have these ritual deeds and words in their hearts. Even as this happens, the way the parish keeps other rituals—infant baptism, first communion, weddings, funerals, Lent and Advent and Eastertide, saints' days—will begin evolving toward participation, toward the work of the people done by heart.

Because this plan begins with Year One's immersion of leadership in preparation, that year is the only commitment required to begin, and the leadership group or groups are the only people who need identifying. Part of the work that year will be decisions on how to organize the following phases of the renewal. Don't expect to find a precise blueprint ("In the eighteenth week of the third year, begin using the cup for communion at all Masses"). That won't happen. The whole reason for the structures of "years" is to emphasize that it is probably best to concentrate on one area at a time. Having learned that, you will do what's best in your parish. The chapters give you materials to work with and refer you to further materials. The expectations are high: Do what was asked at Vatican II in December 1963. But now we know far more about how.

Throughout this book there will be references to many resources from Liturgy Training Publications (LTP). LTP exists to foster the renewal of liturgy mandated by Vatican II. The purpose and format of this book do not allow ignoring resources, and the resources known to and trusted by the author are primarily those of LTP. These will in turn lead to resources from other publishers.

Not much will be said about the structure that a parish uses to prepare for liturgy: preparing for the seasons, developing excellence in ministries, evaluation and development. The basic plan presumes that whether there has been a liturgy committee, a board or an individual responsible, that entity will cooperate fully with the core group as outlined below. It may be that a new structure will develop in the course of the "five years." But this book does not go into the advantages and disadvantages of different structures. It presumes that for anything as drastic as what is envisioned here to happen, the present body will serve in one way or another as an auxiliary to the core group.

Finally, there is one thing you are not allowed to say at any time as you consider this plan or as you begin to engage in this work of renewal: "The people aren't ready." They are.

∾ **Resources** to Gather for Year One

The plan of study outlined in the next chapter for use in Year One requires the following resources. The documents listed here are available in a number of formats and editions. Those marked with an asterisk (*) can be found in the anthology *The Liturgy Documents, Volume One.* Those marked with two asterisks (**) can be found in *The Liturgy Documents, Volume Two.* All resources on this page except two (as noted with a †) are available from Liturgy Training Publications: 1-800-933-1800. These other two publications can be purchased from the United States Catholic Conference: 1-800-235-8722.

Roman Documents

*Constitution on the Sacred Liturgy**

*General Instruction of the Roman Missal**

*General Norms for the Liturgical Year and the Calendar**

*Directory for Masses with Children**

Lectionary for Mass: Introduction*

*Inculturation and the Roman Liturgy****

*Apostolic Letter of Pope John Paul II Dies Domini*** (also available as *Guide to Keeping Sunday Holy,* in English and Spanish)

U.S. Documents

*Music in Catholic Worship**

*Environment and Art in Catholic Worship**

Built of Living Stones †

*Plenty Good Room: The Spirit and Truth of African American Catholic Worship****

*Fulfilled in Your Hearing**

Pastoral Letter of Cardinal Roger Mahony *Gather Faithfully Together* (also available as *Guide for Sunday Mass,* in English and Spanish)

Pastoral Letter of Cardinal Joseph Bernardin *Our Communion, Our Peace, Our Promise* (also available as *Guide for the Assembly,* in English and Spanish)

Short Commentaries on the Documents

Kathleen Hughes, "Overview of the *Constitution on the Sacred Liturgy*"*

Mark Francis, "Overview of *Inculturation and the Roman Liturgy*"**

J-Glenn Murray, "Overview of *Plenty Good Room*"**

Books

Edward Foley, *Preaching Basics*

Gabe Huck, *A Common Sense for Parish Life*

United States Catholic Conference, *Catholic Household Blessings and Prayers* †

Videos

Video Guide to Gather Faithfully Together

From *The Sunday Mass Series: The Roman Catholic Mass Today; We Shall Go Up with Joy; The Word of the Lord; Lift Up Your Hearts; Say Amen! to What You Are*

Year One
Prepare the Leaders to Lead

The difficulty is this: The very beginning is the part you have to figure out for yourself. The notes that follow try to help with goals and resources and major areas to be covered. But beyond that, what practical things can be said? So much depends on the size and history of the parish, on its makeup and location, on the diocese, on the way the liturgy work is now organized, not to mention personalities involved. But few parishes should skip this phase. It builds a foundation for what will be done as the parish, little by little, erects its liturgical dwelling place.

The following sections outline some tasks of this first phase.

Form the Core Group for This Preparation Time

- *The pastor. The pastor need not be the main mover, but he has to be by word and example an enthusiastic participant because of the need for unity and because he is a presider at Sunday liturgy.*

- *The music director. Whether staff or volunteer, the person who has principal responsibility for the music at Sunday liturgy needs the same enthusiasm as the pastor for the project.*

- *The person most responsible for parish liturgy. This may be the liturgy committee chair or a staff person. This person will have connections to the leadership in each ministry.*

- *Those most responsible for parish catechesis. Staff or volunteer, the persons responsible for directing the religious education program, both inside and outside the parish school, both for adults and children, must be involved.*

Depending on the parish experience and structure, there are at least two other people likely to be needed here. One is the chair of the parish council: a non-staff person who serves the whole parish in all its activities. The other is the person (or, in some parishes, the people)—staff or volunteer—who most closely identifies with both parish outreach (service rendered directly to those in need) and parish work for justice. All these people will give shape to the leadership work of Year One. It will help if all have read this book before the initial meeting.

Is it surprising to find the key persons from the catechesis programs needed here? It's high time that it be so, and not because the parish director of religious education is an expert in liturgy or because catechesis of the whole assembly will be an essential part of this program (though catechizing the assembly is a must, and the catechists are essential for this). The catechist sits at the table because of the way we believe the formation of Catholics should take place.

How does one become Christian, become Catholic? The catechist is wholly given to this, but article 14 of the *Constitution on the Sacred Liturgy* quoted earlier names full and conscious and active participation as the *primary and indispensable* source of the authentic Christian spirit. Effective catechesis will draw constantly on the vibrant liturgical life of the parish—not only Sunday eucharist but the sacraments, seasons, saints' festivals and household rituals. Liturgy and catechesis are two distinct ways the church does its work, but they cannot be two independent ways.

A Few Basic Marching Orders for the Core Group

Don't agonize over such things as the location of the tabernacle, postures taken or not taken during various parts of the Mass, or the use or lack of inclusive language. Don't fail to lead, but recognize that even if all these details are handled well, the real work may not have begun.

Don't fuss with the periphery when you still lack a core. Until the Sunday liturgy is strong, almost everything else is a distraction. Admirable as good evening prayer or well-celebrated funerals may be, Sunday eucharist has to hold us to the task.

Don't "stand outside" the assembly. Everyone in the core group must know the liturgy as a member of the Sunday assembly first and must look there for life and nourishment.

Don't try any quick fixes. This is serious work. Be aware of our deep American need to entertain and be entertained, to consume and to feed the consumer. This work of renewal has nothing essential to do with entertaining, novelty, therapy or inspiration. Only when we get beyond that will we have liturgy.

Don't lie to each other, especially when it comes to the responsibilities of presider and homilist. Be polite, but be truthful so that real work for the church can be done.

Likewise, the one who comes from the parish's outreach and justice ministries sits at the table, but not because the task is to turn liturgy into recruitment for many good works. We have figured out this much: The outreach we do and the justice we demand are not the work of a committee. They are the work of a parish. If at liturgy we are being shaped by God into God's reign, then this is where a Catholic is shaped in a "preferential option for the poor" and in how that option is lived. This is where our eyes are trained to interpret the world. This is where we learn our vocabulary and grammar. The liturgical deeds of Sunday—and of the other rites of the church—do not need justice concerns "imposed" on them; indeed, such concerns are essential to the church's liturgy, and so those most involved in outreach and justice need to be at the table to contribute to the discussion.

Some parishes may have one other person (or half a dozen other people) who should be involved from the beginning, but avoid confusing the core group with the larger leadership picture that takes shape during the year.

Chart a Course for the Year

The first task of this core group is to establish what kind of groundwork has to be done before beginning to work with the assembly in Year Two. Consider the following questions and suggested study plan.

- *Who needs to study what during Year One if we are then to begin a period of liturgical renewal in our parish? If, for example, the pastoral letter of Cardinal Mahony,* Gather Faithfully Together, *and the pastoral letter of Cardinal Bernardin,* Our Communion, Our Peace, Our Promise, *are to be the basic texts for the parish liturgical renewal, then this core group should read and discuss these two letters before tackling any of the other tasks described below. (Both are available from LTP, the former titled* Guide for Sunday Mass

List here the names of the core group.

_____

_____

_____

_____

_____

_____

_____

_____

_____

_____

_____

and the latter Guide for the Assembly. Guide for the Assembly *includes a thorough discussion guide geared to various groups. Both books are available in English and Spanish.)*

- *How can the core group and others become more familiar this year with the basic documents on the liturgy, beginning with the* Constitution on the Sacred Liturgy? *(The most basic of these are found in* The Liturgy Documents: Volume One, *which is also available in Spanish;* The Liturgy Documents: Volume Two *is available only in English. Both are available from LTP. Overviews and outlines are included for each document.) One possible way of organizing this reading and discussion is suggested in the accompanying sidebar on page 21. The tone of these discussions should be eager and enthusiastic. They need not be practical at this point. The goal here is a well-informed, articulate and enthusiastic leadership. This takes time, and there are no real shortcuts.*

- *How are each of these leaders to involve their "constituents" during this preparation period? In other words, how is the pastor to involve the parish staff, parish council and all ordained priests who regularly preside at the Sunday liturgy? How is the music director to involve all cantors and choir members and instrumentalists? How are those responsible for catechesis to involve the catechists who work with children? How is the liturgy director to involve the leaders of each ministry and eventually the ministers themselves? All of this begins during Year One, before the assembly as a whole is engaged in catechesis and development of its Sunday liturgy. The goal here is not necessarily to involve every staff member, every catechist, every minister. The goal is to create a broad base for the work of the next four years. How to do this will vary greatly.*

- *When and how do we recognize that the liturgy cannot be separated from outreach and justice efforts in which the parish is involved? What persons represent this ministry, and how are they to be involved in this time of laying foundations?*

Discussions of music and of matters related to the physical setting for worship will certainly surface over the course of these sessions. The team may want to add two separate discussions to give these areas specific attention. *Music in Catholic Worship* and *Environment and Art in Catholic Worship* would form the basis of these discussions respectively.

This series of discussions is ambitious in any parish. It won't be easy to find time. In most parishes it will only happen when the importance given to this work allows the staff and others to put something else aside so that each participant can give adequate time to reading, meeting and discussing.

It is difficult enough to find time for the reading, but one thing even more difficult is strongly suggested here: Ask each member of the core group not only to do the reading for each session but to write down some reflections as well. This could be two paragraphs or a "web" (a diagram or flowchart or outline) of thoughts and questions and ways of exploring the subject. This writing is not an exercise in applying the reading ("Here at Saint X, we could implement this by . . ."). It's primary purpose is to get people thinking. As several wise people have said, "I don't know what I think until I see what I'm going to say." Finding out what we think should happen in quiet time before the meeting. The written pieces need not be read aloud, though they could be, but each participant could receive a copy of every other participant's notes.

Leadership in the discussions may be rotated among the members unless one person has a gift for this. What is being sought here is a body of knowledge so that a group can become well versed in the documents. However, there is a danger of simply skimming along, nodding and saying, "Yes, we do all of that here." That response should probably be challenged. Go deeper. Look harder at parish practice. The leader's task, and the group's task, is not to let each other off easy. Probe and challenge.

A Reading and Study Plan

The next few pages outline a study plan that may be useful for the core group or for any broader group (drawn from the catechists, the liturgy committee, the staff, the parish council, the peace and justice committee) that the core group invites to be part of the preparation. It uses the organization of *Gather Faithfully Together* (LTP's *Guide for Sunday Mass*) as a structure for 11 discussions, noting appropriate readings from the basic documents to go with each.

These discussions must occur at least once each month or the group will lose continuity. If the core leadership group meets weekly for a staff meeting, this discussion could be 30 minutes each week until all the readings are discussed. Or each discussion could be its own meeting of approximately two hours. Do the reading *before* each discussion.

Remember that this is an overview, a time to work for common understandings of the renewal, not a time to restructure the parish's present practice. (That begins in Year Two.)

All of the resources suggested for the following discussions are listed on page 15. Number references to each resource refer to article numbers in the documents, unless otherwise noted.

<table>
<tr><td>

Date: _____

Time: _____

</td><td>

Discussion 1
Vatican II: What Is the Mandate for Liturgical Renewal?

Gather Faithfully Together (Guide for Sunday Mass), 1–17

Our Communion, Our Peace, Our Promise (Guide for the Assembly), 1–21

Constitution on the Sacred Liturgy, 1–46, with overview by Kathleen Hughes, pages 2–6 in *The Liturgy Documents, Volume One*

General Instruction of the Roman Missal, 1–15

Music in Catholic Worship, 1–9

Environment and Art in Catholic Worship, 1–8

</td></tr>
</table>

<table>
<tr><td>

Date: _____

Time: _____

</td><td>

Discussion 2
Sunday

Guide for Sunday Mass, 18–23

Constitution on the Sacred Liturgy, 106

General Norms for the Liturgical Year and the Calendar, 4–7

Dies Domini (Guide to Keeping Sunday Holy)
The entire document could be read, but especially the first two chapters.

</td></tr>
</table>

Evaluate the Present

This step is an addition to (or a part of) the above study for some brave parishes, and for others it will be a shorter but less complete alternative.

Having read the two pastoral letters of Cardinals Bernardin and Mahony, and whatever other materials have been identified as a point of departure for the work ahead, the core group looks carefully at Sunday practice as it is now. This is not yet a detailed recommendation for shaping a renewal but a critique in light of what is glimpsed in the letters.

It may be helpful if, in addition to the pastoral letters, the group views a number of videos on the Sunday Mass: *Video Guide to Gather Faithfully Together,* along with the five-part video series on Sunday Mass called, naturally, *The Sunday Mass Series,* would be good for this and can be used over and over again by various groups in the implementation phases. The videos in the series were made with four assemblies at their regular Sunday Masses; they also include interviews with parishioners and staff that are extremely revealing. What the videos show is not a blueprint for any other parish but four committed parishes in the process of making their Sunday liturgy a strong center of the whole parish's life.

	Discussion 5
Date: _____	**The Assembly: Full, Conscious and Active Participation**
	Guide for Sunday Mass, 88–100, 122–25
Time: _____	*Constitution on the Sacred Liturgy,* 14
	General Instruction of the Roman Missal, 62–64
	Guide to Keeping Sunday Holy, 42–51
	Environment and Art in Catholic Worship, 9, 27–32
	Built of Living Stones, 51–53
	Music in Catholic Worship, 15–18

	Discussion 6
Date: _____	**The Presider and the Various Ministers**
	Guide for Sunday Mass, 101–4, 129–44
Time: _____	*General Instruction of the Roman Missal,* 59–61
	Lectionary for Mass: Introduction, 38–57
	Directory for Masses with Children, 22–24
	Music in Catholic Worship, 35–38
	Environment and Art in Catholic Worship, 12–26
	Fulfilled in Your Hearing, 16–24

This evaluation of present Sunday practice need not get bogged down in solving problems yet. There is certainly room to raise and record a variety of great and small problems, but the focus here is more on the whole. Use the following groups of questions in your discussion.

• *With what mentality, what attitudes, what expectations, do people now approach the Sunday liturgy? This includes presider and musician and ministers, but it also includes the rest of the assembly. Much can be known from observation: how people enter, when they enter, where they take their places, their attentiveness, singing and silence.*

Discussion 7
Catechesis and the Liturgy, Catechesis for the Liturgy

Date: _____

Guide for Sunday Mass, 145–59

Time: _____

Directory for Masses with Children, 1–15

See also *A Common Sense for Parish Life* (LTP) described below, and the introduction to *Catholic Household Blessings and Prayers.*

Discussion 8
The Seasons of the Liturgical Year and Ordinary Time

Date: _____

Constitution on the Sacred Liturgy, 102–11

Time: _____

General Norms for the Liturgical Year and the Calendar, 17–47

Lectionary for Mass: Introduction, 58–68

Built of Living Stones, 122–29

• *On a scale of 1 to 10, where would you put yourselves if asked: Are people here to* do *(10) or to* be *done to (1)? What do we, the leadership, expect of people by way of preparation and participation? What does the assembly expect of itself in preparation and participation? This is where the videos can be helpful. Equally helpful would be a few visits to parishes that have worked hard in developing good liturgy.*

• *Discuss the preaching, although this may be difficult.* Preaching Basics *by Ed Foley explores what "liturgical preaching" is meant to be. Is this your expectation? How preaching is prepared and done can be examined much later in this process, but here it is important to determine whether the parish's preachers are "imbued" with the spirit of the liturgy and capable of articulating that spirit.*

• *This evaluation should extend, in a general way, to the ministers. How are they prepared? Is there a rotation out of a ministry after a few years? Why or why not? Who watches out to commend or suggest better ways to ministers? What leadership is there, and is it restricted to scheduling?*

<table>
<tr><td>Date:

Time:</td><td>**Discussion 9**
Liturgy, Outreach, Justice: Sunday Mass and Christian Life

Guide for Sunday Mass, 105–10

Guide for the Assembly, 53, 70, 87–88

Guide to Keeping Sunday Holy, 45, 55–73</td></tr>
</table>

<table>
<tr><td>Date:

Time:</td><td>**Discussion 10**
The Liturgy in the Context of Culture: Inculturation

Guide for Sunday Mass, 27–35

Constitution on the Sacred Liturgy, 37–40

Inculturation and the Roman Liturgy, with the overview by Mark Francis, pages 108–12 in *The Liturgy Documents, Volume Two*

Plenty Good Room: The Spirit and Truth of African American Catholic Worship, with overview by J-Glenn Murray, pages 158–62 in *The Liturgy Documents, Volume Two*

Built of Living Stones, 38–45</td></tr>
</table>

Discover What Binds Liturgy, Catechesis and Justice

This is built into the discussions above, but more time may be needed to make it applicable to parish practice. In many parishes, a serious but mostly undiscussed problem is the separation of liturgy and catechesis. Sometimes they are like two independent units, each off and running on its own (but occasionally facing off to argue about sacramental preparation).

One task of this phase is to put all that on the table and come away with a notion of how vital these two are to parish life and how intertwined they are meant to be. *A Common Sense for Parish Life* (LTP) is a workbook that invites a group like this one, or the whole parish staff, to work their way together through a number of statements, examining themselves on each one, struggling for a way forward. The challenge

Guide for Sunday Mass, 80–86, 170–185
Although this is dated and intended for the archdiocese of
    Los Angeles, it will help the leadership think very concretely
    about implementation.

Guide for the Assembly, 80–86
See also pages 29–58 of *Guide for the Assembly,* discussion
    questions and resources.

is to achieve some common understandings of how Christian
formation happens.

These are the ten statements that participants are asked to
struggle with and dialogue about in *Common Sense* (each
statement comes with various exercises to help the group
probe their own experience and direction):

- *We believe that creation, humanity and human deeds always
  hold and reveal the presence of God. This sacramental
  stance is the foundation of our way of living in the world.*

- *The life of a parish is manifest in: attending to God's word,
  interceding, praising and giving thanks to God at the Sunday
  eucharist and in prayer and ritual of many kinds (worship);
  forming members—young and old, new and veteran—
  through many ways of teaching (catechesis); building up the
  body of Christ, the church (community); witnessing to justice and caring for all those in need (service).*

- *Scripture is integral to liturgy as well as to every aspect of
  parish life.*

- *Sacramental life and celebration flourish when all parish
  ministers, especially those responsible for catechesis and
  liturgy, work together and share a vision.*

- *Catechesis for all ages takes place within the community in a
  great variety of settings. In catechesis we are challenged and
  enabled to ponder, to question and to draw one another on in
  understanding and zeal for the gospel.*

- *Liturgy and catechesis bring the power of the gospel into the very heart of culture and cultures.*

- *Sunday eucharist is the central action of parish life. It has a vital relationship to all parish activities and especially to the daily lives of all the baptized.*

- *The sacraments are the normal actions and celebrations of the assembly, which is all the baptized persons of a parish. The parish itself, then, is the primary symbol because it is the church, the body of Christ, that transacts the sacraments. We believe and we act not as individuals but as the church and even as this church, this parish.*

- *The church's liturgical year organizes the sacramental work of the parish.*

- *The celebration of the liturgy, supported by lifelong study, leads to the doing of justice.*

At least two important things can happen when these questions are honestly addressed. First, the group can make progress in putting aside old models of how parish life is lived. This would include a clerical model where all power and decisions rest with the pastor, but it would also include the more contemporary "corporate" model that sees the pastor as a sort of chief executive officer surrounded by the vice president for religious education, the vice president for youth, and so on. Second, the group can move toward renewal of the Sunday liturgy with some shared sense for how liturgy is not a universe unto itself but connected and vital to the realms of catechesis, justice, community and outreach.

Decide What's Next

All of the above are now brought to bear on the remaining phases of the renewal of parish liturgy. If the core group has read the remainder of this book, it is now time to decide whether this process will work in this parish. Do we undertake four more "years" or phases in the order they are given here, or in some other order?

By this time in Year One, many of the "constituents" of the core group will also be involved and will be ready to move. Their roles should be clear as the leadership now invites the whole parish to begin this renewal.

One caution is in order. Through all the next phases, it may be wise to suspend any other extraordinary programs that are meant to involve large groups of parishioners: RENEW, adult study programs and the like. Talk about this now and about the temptation that will come from various sources along the way. Stay focused.

A Way to Go

There are, in esence, five steps that need to be taken in the work of the next four years (or whatever phases you choose). These are:

Read and study

Plan changes

Train the ministers

Catechize the assembly

Implement the changes

These five labels will appear throughout the rest of the book to indicate the passages designed to help in each step.

∾ **Resources** to Gather for Year Two

All of these resources are available from Liturgy Training Publications: 1-800-933-1800. Those marked with an asterisk (*) can be found in the anthology *The Liturgy Documents, Volume One.*

Roman Documents

*General Instruction of the Roman Missal**

U.S. Documents

Pastoral Letter of Cardinal Roger Mahony *Gather Faithfully Together* (also available as *Guide for Sunday Mass,* in English and Spanish)

Pastoral Letter of Cardinal Joseph Bernardin *Our Communion, Our Peace, Our Promise* (also available as *Guide for the Assembly,* in English and Spanish)

Books

Gabe Huck, *The Communion Rite at Sunday Mass*

Lawrence Mick, *Guide for Ushers*

Gabe Huck, *Preaching about the Mass*

David Philippart, editor, *Basket, Basin, Plate and Cup: Vessels in the Liturgy*

David Philippart, *Saving Signs, Wondrous Words*

Victoria M. Tufano, *Guide for Ministers of Communion* (in English and Spanish)

Videos

Video Guide to Gather Faithfully Together

Say Amen! to What You Are (part five of *The Sunday Mass Series)*

Video Guide for Ministers of Communion

Year Two
The Communion Rite

A parish could begin with any part of Sunday Mass. The communion rite is suggested for several reasons that will have some validity in many parishes:

* *The way it is currently done needs improvement.*

* *Improvements to the communion rite make a great difference, which is usually well received.*

* *Catechesis then comes easier, is more concrete and is more widely appreciated.*

* *After work on the communion rite is completed, it is easier then to continue with other parts of the liturgy.*

Here is a general approach to this year's work to renew the communion rite:

* *Using some of the resources listed below (and on page 30), and using this chapter itself as a starting point, the core group explores the rite: history, ministries involved, present practice, other possibilities. It may be best in the first discussion to take an introductory look at the rite as a whole from these various perspectives, then spend other sessions focused on one or two elements, for example, the Lord's*

Prayer and the peace greeting. An important element in these discussions will be mystagogy: discovering how people can speak from their own experience about the mystery we celebrate and allowing them to do so. Discussions should be held at least once a month. Along the way, only this chapter itself need be read by all the participants. Other reading can be divided: different people read from different resources and then report to the whole group. Remember, it won't work to skip the homework. Reading must inform the discussion.

- *These discussions lead naturally to imagining the way the rite can best be done Sunday by Sunday in the parish. Someone should be making notes all along of practical (even conflicting) ideas that spring up during the discussions. These are then available when the group begins its practical deliberations: Can we envision our renewed communion rite, and can we envision the steps we must take to get there?*

- *With this process, resources and occasions for catechesis for the whole parish must be explored. This is focused primarily on how the assembly as a whole can be drawn into the discussion, asked to read and ponder, and addressed in the homily. But it also involves more direct work with those in the ministries: ministers of communion, acolytes, ushers, musicians, presiders. The lectionary and the liturgical year are always available as resources as the group makes its plans. Questions like these will come up during the process: When will be the right moment to talk in the homily about posture during the Lord's Prayer and whether the prayer is normally sung or recited? When and how can changes in the way the communion procession is done be addressed? When and how will parishioners be invited to join in after-Mass discussions that focus on all the implications of receiving from the cup, and what practices at Mass will enhance this?*

- *When the assembly and ministers have been engaged in catechesis and discussion, are we then ready for implementation of the new order? Should the changes be implemented all at once or one element at a time? What bulletin or other written materials will be needed?*

- *Finally, great attention to the ministers and to the flow of the liturgy is needed as implementation begins. Patience is needed, too: It can take many Sundays before this takes hold and all are at home.*

Resources

The following are the basic resources, the essentials. They can lead to others. The first of these, *The Communion Rite at Sunday Mass,* should be read one section at a time as the core group works its way through the communion rite. The second, a video, should be viewed several times in the course of the discussions, always with time to question and discuss, particularly to attend to specific remarks made by parishioners on the video. Consider also how this video will be useful in working with communion ministers, musicians and the whole assembly. All the resources listed below are available from Liturgy Training Publications.

Read and study

Gabe Huck, *The Communion Rite at Sunday Mass*

This is a careful consideration of each element of the communion rite. Sidebars provide history, theology, bulletin inserts and many other resources. This is also a guide to the official documentation about the communion rite.

Assigned to:

_____

_____

_____

All will benefit from watching *Say Amen! to What You Are.* This is a 30-minute video (part five of *The Sunday Mass Series)* that visits the Sunday assembly at St. Henry's Church in Cleveland, Ohio. It shows how the communion rite can become the work of all present, and we hear the wisdom of parishioners and staff as they reflect on each moment within the rite. The discussion guide that accompanies the video provides help for its use with various groups.

Appropriate sections of the following general resources used in Year One should also be reviewed:

Assigned to:	*General Instruction of the Roman Missal,* 56k, 110–27, 240–52
_____	*Gather Faithfully Together (Guide for Sunday Mass),* 69–77, 164–69
_____	*Video Guide to Gather Faithfully Together* Review with special attention to how the communion rite unfolds.
_____	*Our Communion, Our Peace, Our Promise (Guide for the Assembly),* 65–73, and relevant sections of the discussion guide

Some brief passages from other books will also be helpful. They could be assigned and read together.

Assigned to:	*Preaching about the Mass,* "The Liturgy of the Eucharist II," pages 42–51
_____	*Saving Signs, Wondrous Words,* "The Lifting Up of My Hands," pages 41–43; "Let Us Offer Each Other a Sign of Peace," pages 48–51; "Take and Drink," pages 52–55
_____	*Basket, Basin, Plate and Cup,* read chapters that appeal to you
_____	

Remember, the above readings can be divided up among the members of the core group, with those who do the reading reporting to the rest during the course of the discussions. But the entire core group should read the rest of this chapter.

When it comes time to work directly with the ministers, see these resources: *Guide for Ushers* by Lawrence Mick, *Guide for Ministers of Communion* by Victoria M. Tufano, and *Video Guide for Ministers of Communion.*

The Communion Rite: An Overview

We do well to have something as simple as this to guide us: *Plan changes* When we have finished praising and thanking God around our table, over the simple but so lovely bread and wine that become for us the body and blood of Christ, then we take a deep breath (because the eucharistic prayer itself has been intense and exhausting), and we pray the dearest, hardest prayer we know, the Lord's Prayer. Then we turn to one and all alike, and we embrace or kiss or clasp hands and say, "Peace!" and "Christ's peace!" Here, moments before we share the bread and wine, we give a sign of what that communion means: Here there is no first place and no last place, but all have the same place. Today is God's reign, some little bit of it, among us.

And when that ends, we attend again to the table, and we see the gesture that gave this gathering of Christians its earliest name, the breaking of the bread. While this happens, we sing a litany that has us praying for mercy and for peace, praying to Jesus under the beautiful name "Lamb of God" and other names that come from the scriptures. And when all the bread is broken and ready, when all the wine has been poured into cups for us, the presider proclaims what this bread and wine is, and offers an invitation: "This is the Lamb of God . . ." And we say, "Lord, I am not worthy . . ." And we are not. No one is. And that is exactly why we then come forward, singing and processing together, to eat a morsel of the holy bread and to drink from the cup. We receive what we are, the body of Christ and the blood of Christ.

Afterward, the whole assembly is quiet for some time, then we pray that what we have done here may be reflected in every word and gesture of life, to which we say, "Amen!"

That is the communion rite.

We must have such a simple flow, such an order, such an image in our minds at all times as we think about the eventual way this rite is enacted Sunday after Sunday in a parish.

What Is the Purpose of the Communion Rite?

The *General Instruction of the Roman Missal* speaks of the communion rite in this way:

> *Since the eucharistic celebration is the paschal meal, it is right that the faithful who are properly disposed receive the Lord's body and blood as spiritual food as he commanded. This is the purpose of the breaking of the bread and the other preparatory rites that lead directly to the communion of the people. (GIRM, 56)*

Note what is said here: The communion rite is the taking and eating, the taking and drinking, by the assembly. All that comes before—Lord's Prayer, peace, breaking, litany—has that communion as its goal. That should give us perspective on how we enact the rite.

This description in the *General Instruction* also makes clear what we have often obscured in parish practice: Who does this rite? The church! This assembly! Who prays the Our Father? Who gives the peace? Who sings the Lamb of God litany? Who makes the procession and sings the procession? Who eats and who drinks? Who keeps still for a while? Who says "amen" to ratify the rite?

Especially in the communion rite, it is clear who does the liturgy, and it is clear that those who minister are part of the assembly who render some simple and quite limited service. Anything done by these ministers to turn the assembly into an audience, into "those for whom the liturgy is being done," contradicts the plain dictates of the liturgy documents and common sense. Our every effort in renewing the parish's communion rite must keep this in mind. In the end, it will be the assembly's rite, and it will be strong enough and beautiful enough to be the treasure of that assembly Sunday after Sunday, year after year.

The Lord's Prayer

If the doxology and the Great Amen of the eucharistic prayer have been a climax to that prayer, if the presider has held the bread and cup through the Amen, then there is a moment to place the vessels on the altar and so in silence to mark an end to one deed and to face another.

The words of invitation are direct and need no elaboration whatsoever. The presider—who throughout the eucharistic prayer spoke not to the assembly but for the assembly and with the assembly in a kind of proclamatory dialogue—now speaks to the assembly (last done when inviting, "Lift up your hearts" and "Let us proclaim the mystery of faith"). The presider addresses the assembly, using the good words in the sacramentary (four variations are given). This is done from memory, eyes on those being invited to pray and not on the book. Then the presider does whatever is necessary so that his voice is not heard above others in the prayer itself.

The Lord's Prayer is our daily prayer, the prayer we give to catechumens when we want to tell them how we pray. This happens only in the last weeks before baptism. (Those catechumens, even if they have become "the elect" during Lent, are not here at this moment at Sunday liturgy; they were dismissed after the homily.) The Lord's Prayer is how Christians pray. It contains the whole of Christian spirituality and hope for the future. It is a prayer whose images come thoroughly from the psalms and from the Hebrew scriptures (from where else could Jesus have drawn it?).

Is the prayer chanted? Yes, and always with the same tone, a tone that will not leave anyone out. It is not a hymn, not a folk song. The common chant version might be one of the few pieces of song that every English-speaking Catholic knows; other languages have comparable settings. Whether to sing or recite at the parish's Sunday liturgy should depend not a bit on the presider or the cantor. We always do it, or we never do it. We do not put the assembly at the whim of anyone here. Its members need not wait for cues from anyone. The presider chants the invitation, the assembly chants the prayer.

Because the presider's "Deliver us . . . " and the assembly's "For the kingdom . . . " are not separate from the Lord's Prayer, the chant continues through these. When presiders chant the "Deliver us . . ." they are less likely to add their own embellishments to the generally fine text in the sacramentary.

The importance of posture and gesture are clear if we see what parish practice has done with the Lord's Prayer in the last 30 years. Many assemblies are completely at home joining hands for this prayer. Even if revised rubrics call on the assembly to assume the *orans* posture (hands raised and open, the posture taken by the presider), assemblies accustomed to joining hands should at least be invited to learn about this alternative posture and to dialogue about whether to make such a change. In assemblies where there has been no custom of joining hands, the *orans* posture can be introduced with good catechesis.

The Kiss of Peace

The prayer that begins "Lord Jesus Christ..." is best said quietly so it leads to but does not compete with what comes next. In this prayer the presider is not addressing the assembly, not making a speech, not seeking another place for improvisation. It should be quiet and prayed as written. Then the "peace" is spoken by the presider to the assembly with eye contact and an open gesture, just as every greeting in the liturgy is. And the invitation or exhortation, almost a command, of the deacon or presider follows immediately upon the assembly's response: "Let us offer each other the sign of peace."

The liturgy clearly emphasizes the formal greeting ("The peace of the Lord be with you always") and not the exhortation.

It seems to presume that the greeting is enough and the exchange could begin at once. But because we have become accustomed to the rhythm of the exhortation before we exchange the peace, it is probably best to retain it as an urgent and direct address to the assembly.

The kiss of peace has been seen as a gesture of forgiveness, a gesture of reverence for each other, an affirmation of the unity we are ever seeking. We need not choose a "meaning" for what we do here; doing it well will bring forth many meanings. Perhaps we would do well to retain the name "the kiss of peace" rather than "peace greeting" or even "sign of peace," though these are both good names. In our liturgy there is kissing of the altar and of the gospel book at every Mass. And with these we have this kiss of peace, the kiss we give one another.

The kiss of peace involves the body, and the gesture is exchanged between two persons. This moment demands the homilist speak of it now and then, not because people need correction but because all, homilist included, need to ponder over and over the meaning of what we do here. Consider this bit of pondering in *Saving Signs, Wondrous Words:*

> *When we offer each other a sign of* Christ's *peace, we are saying with our bodies that we hold dear the One who is our peace. We are believing with our bodies that the barriers between us have been broken down, the divisions undone, the ruptures repaired. We are pledging with our action that we will leave this place and spread this peace of Christ to the sidewalks and the supermarket aisles. . . . That dream of peace is born here, in this assembly, in handshakes and hugs offered around this table, in this hour. So when we come to the sign of peace, know who you are and what it is that you do.*
>
> *Turn to the person next to you, in front of you, behind you. Clasp hands or hug that person as you would embrace Christ himself, for indeed that is what you are doing. And receive from that person the peace of Christ, for that, in fact, is what it is.*

The Kiss of Peace

Write here your impressions of how the kiss of peace is shared at Sunday Mass in this parish. (It may be different at different Mass times.)

_____

_____

_____

_____

_____

_____

_____

_____

_____

_____

_____

_____

_____

_____

_____

_____

_____

_____

_____

_____

_____

_____

And clasp, *don't* shake *hands. Use both hands, and hold them for a moment, without pumping them. Look into each other's eyes.*

Don't let this holy moment slip by you as though you were a robot going through the motions. Don't share this holy moment only with those whom you know and like. It isn't necessary to greet everyone in the room, either, but do reach broadly. (page 49, 50)

Nothing shows the absurdity of so many of our worship spaces like this dilemma: Should the presider go to greet the assembly during the peace? Go? Go? Why isn't the presider in the midst of the assembly so that such a question could never occur to us? But whatever the space, presiders and acolytes and (most certainly!) ushers should be quiet models of what happens here: the embrace, the hand clasp, given willy-nilly to all who are near.

Greeting "all who are near" is important. The point of the peace is the point of the assembly of the baptized: The bond we have in belonging to Christ is stronger than the bond that joins me to my parent, my spouse, my child, my friend. Within arm's reach of me, at Mass, should be people who don't fall into any of those categories. We have to open our eyes and recognize this amazing bond we the baptized have with one another, and far from making our parish into or speaking of our parish as a warm and homogenous "family," we need to see in ourselves at liturgy exactly the variety that makes up our church: age and sex and sexual orientation and wealth and education and politics. We need the variety, and that's what the peace is all about. This is no longer a domestic model. It is the church! That's always going to shatter the would-be coziness of the family.

This kiss of peace, like the intercessions and the eucharistic prayer and the communion itself, was once something forbidden to the catechumens. Only the baptized could do this, *had* to do this. There was a deep understanding in such practice.

The Breaking of the Bread

Communion ministers may come to the table after the Amen of the eucharistic prayer (thus providing more of a pause between the eucharistic prayer and the communion rite), or during the peace greeting (exchanging the peace with others as they come forward, but not after the Lamb of God begins). Till now there has been a single plate on the table, and a single large vessel or perhaps a large cup and a flagon, both filled. As the peace greeting concludes, acolytes and communion ministers bring empty plates and cups from the side table to the altar. They do not begin to break or pour at once.

When the kiss of peace has finished, or even to bring it to a conclusion, the presider lifts up a loaf of the consecrated bread and breaks it. The singing of the Lamb of God begins as the bread is broken; it continues as long as it takes to prepare for the holy communion, then concludes when the presider is ready to speak the invitation: "This is the Lamb of God." The Lamb of God—both words and melody—should be so familiar that the assembly can always join in the repeated refrains without help of any book or other aid.

Respect for the good order of the liturgy would seem to dictate something like this: When, as is ideal, all or some of the bread consecrated has been in a single or several large loaves, presider and one or more other ministers break this into smaller pieces as the litany continues. If there are no more than six cups to be filled, one minister can do this from the flagon. When all are filled, that minister hands them one at a time to the waiting ministers. The same is done with the consecrated bread: one minister fills the plates, then gives one to each minister. When there are more cups and plates, another minister should help the one pouring, removing each filled cup and handing it to a minister.

As the ministers receive their vessels, they face the assembly, either remaining around the table or going at once to their stations. The ministers receive communion last.

The above practice presumes several things that unfortunately still are not true in many parishes:

- *During this time, no one ever goes to the tabernacle. The rubrics make this clear. The basic integrity of this assembly's eucharist demands it. A discussion of this can be found in* The Communion Rite at Sunday Mass, *pages 43–45 and pages 76–77.*

- *At every Mass, communion is shared in both kinds, bread and cup. The sign of communion is more complete when given under both kinds, since the sign of the eucharistic meal appears more clearly. The intention of Christ that the new and eternal covenant be ratified in his blood is better expressed, as is the relationship of the eucharistic banquet to the heavenly banquet (see the* General Instruction of the Roman Missal, *240).*

  For more on the sharing and meaning of the cup, see The Communion Rite at Sunday Mass, *pages 32–35, 37, 42–43, 46–48, 52–54, 58–59 and 68–71. Many questions and problems are dealt with in these pages. There are many opportunities in the course of the liturgical year when the homily can reflect on the wine and on sharing from the cup. The invitation needs to be renewed again and again until participation is the norm.*

- *At every Mass, there is bread to break.* The General Instruction of the Roman Missal *is clear: "The nature of the sign demands that the material for the eucharistic celebration appear as actual food" (GIRM, 283). For wine to appear as actual food, the quantity must say to all: You are welcome, you are expected, at this cup. For the bread to appear as actual food, there must be something that resembles bread as we know it in our lives. Today we know unleavened bread as bread. But do the hosts used in many parishes meet this criterion? For more on the bread, see* The Communion Rite at Sunday Mass, *pages 41, 60–66, 78.*

- *The vessels meet criteria of quality and appropriateness. All the vessels used should be seen as treasures of the community, not as personal possessions of the presider. For more, see* The Communion Rite at Sunday Mass, *pages 44, 47. These too can be spoken of in preaching. They are ways to understand the bond between this table and all the tables where we gather and take delight in one another and nourishment from God's gifts. The vessels are handled with the greatest reverence. Communion ministers and presiders should be people who have a sense for this.*

The Procession

When all are in place except the presider and one minister (who remain at the altar), the Lamb of God ends and immediately the presider lifts the cup and a piece of the consecrated bread and speaks the invitation: "This is the Lamb of God . . ." All respond, "Lord, I am not worthy . . .," and immediately three things happen:

- *The presider takes holy communion, first the bread, then the cup.*

- *At the very same time, immediately after "Lord, I am not worthy . . .," the communion song begins.*

- *Then the assembly begins receiving communion. The presider and the remaining minister of the cup come to their stations after the presider's communion.*

Nothing would seem to prohibit the presider from ministering the cup rather than the bread, and a deacon is expected to be minister of the cup.

Though the words of the presider's invitation to holy communion, "Happy are those who are called to his supper," may vary, they should always be brief and direct, and end in a way that draws the assembly's response, "Lord, I am not worthy . . ."

How does the assembly come to this holy communion? We speak of a procession but generally settle for lining up. Procession is the notion that fits what is happening here: the eucharistic banquet, the *sacrum convivium,* the holy banquet, the image of the heavenly feast and of God's reign, the supper of the Lamb. This is the welcome table imagined in the African American spiritual: "Gonna' sit at that welcome table one of these days." We have to know what's going on here because of the way it sounds, the way it moves, the way it feels. It isn't the line at a fast-food place. We are not lining up. We are in procession. There's no comparison.

What helps?

- *It helps if the people all process in the same direction, toward the table.*

- *It helps if the assembly can move. That is a function of the number of communion ministers and the work of the ushers.*

- *It helps if the music is strong walking music, sung "by heart": psalms and refrains are the best of the tradition. It need not literally describe what is happening.*

- *It helps if this procession begins during the singing of the Lamb of God, if it starts not from the front and center positions, but from the far sides and goes around the back and up the center. It helps, that is, when the initial movement surrounds the assembly.*

- *It helps if the assembly observes the rubrics on posture and stands for the entire reception of holy communion, until all have received, and then all are seated at the same time.*

Paradoxically, achieving this sense of the church as the sacred banquet, singing and processing as we surround our table, makes possible the most personal moment of the liturgy: standing face-to-face with the minister, proclaiming "Amen," and receiving the body and blood of the Lord.

Making a procession rather than a line-up is a challenge. Much thought and even experimentation are usually needed to find the best solution for where the procession begins and how it flows. Ushers are important in beginning and continuing the procession and also in giving good example as they themselves receive bread and cup at the end of the procession. *The Communion Rite at Sunday Mass* has many suggestions on working within the limits of various floor plans to achieve a communion procession; see pages 60–74.

When all have received (including any who cannot come forward), one by one the ministers come to the side table where the vessels are to be left. Those who come first to this table offer communion to the others. When they have received themselves, they cover all the vessels with a clean cloth and return to their places. The presider returns to the chair, but would normally wait to sit until all the communion ministers are back in their places so all can sit down at the same time.

The Time after the Procession

When all have taken communion, including the ministers of communion, the singing concludes. The rubrics call for some silence now or for singing a hymn of thanksgiving. Most will opt for the former, with the entire assembly sitting down together for a lengthy silence. All the ministers as well need to keep this still time. This concludes when the presider rises, and all rise, for the prayer after communion. The Amen of the assembly concludes the communion rite. Only then it is time for the announcements and the business of the week.

The Ministries

Train the ministers

In its work, the core group needs to work not only toward the shape of the rite but also toward the preparation of all the ministers involved and of the whole assembly. Various materials exist for general preparation and continued renewal of the ministers, so here are a few points for emphasis when these ministers are prepared for their service in the renewed liturgy of the communion rite. It is always a good idea to ask that all ministers read and discuss together a basic text, such as the first parts of *Gather Faithfully Together.*

The Presider

Presiding, especially in the communion rite, is not dominating. The rite, when all know it by heart, will flow from the energy and sense of all in the assembly. This is as it should be. The presider should try hard to work within this dynamic, to learn pace and timing that serve the prayer of the church. To facilitate this the presider should do the following.

- *Give the invitations well (to join in the Lord's Prayer, to share the kiss of peace, to come to the table, to pray the concluding prayer) and expect that the assembly will accept and do what is invited.*

- *Do not dominate the Lord's Prayer or any other text that is spoken or chanted together. The presider is to say, "Lord, I am not worthy . . ." with the assembly, but as with all texts, the presider's voice should not be heard above the voices of others. The prayer "May the body and blood of Christ . . ." is never to be said aloud.*

- *Break the bread with great reverence, and receive the body and blood of Christ with the same reverence.*

- *During the procession, give yourself entirely to attending to each person who comes before you.*

- *Make your posture that of the assembly. Do not sit until the ministers have returned to their places and the song has come to its conclusion.*

- *Do not rush to the concluding prayer. Silence, stillness, is needed here. Then stand and, if needed, gesture for all to stand. Never speak directions about posture.*

- *Do not impose some private piety on the liturgy or on the assembly. Instead, immerse yourself in the piety of the liturgy.*

The Musicians

The communion rite is, like most liturgy, sung. It is sung by the assembly in dialogue with the presider (for the Lord's Prayer and its doxology), with the cantor (for the Lamb of God), and with whatever back and forth there may be in the communion song. Finally, a song of thanksgiving is an alternative to the silent time after communion.

There is the matter of timing:

- *The Lord's Prayer and its conclusion ("For the kingdom . . .") flow in dialogue with the presider.*

- *The Lamb of God begins as the presider raises the bread and breaks it. It concludes only when all ministers are in place and the presider is ready to say, "This is the lamb of God . . ."*

- *The communion song should begin immediately after the response "Lord, I am not worthy . . ." is finished. Any delay (for example, while the choir takes communion, or even a 30-second delay while music is shifted around) works against the sense of procession. This single song concludes only when all have taken holy communion.*

When these matters of timing are not done with consistency (for example, one week the communion song begins at once, the next week it begins after the choir's communion) the assembly is, in effect, being told that their liturgy is subject to the whim of their ministers. This should not be so.

There is also the matter of repertoire:

- *The assembly would normally have only one chant for the Lord's Prayer that is used throughout the year, including the seasons and feasts. When the presider simply cannot intone the Lord's Prayer, the cantor may need to come in with the first note right after the presider finishes the spoken invitation.*

- *The assembly might know a few versions of the Lamb of God, possibly assigned to different seasons. But a single version might also be very acceptable. This is a ritual element where a strong melody, one that deepens with repetition, can serve week after week, much like the single chant for the Lord's Prayer. This strength is what matters, and it must be the strength of a litany, that genre where there is a call-and-response rhythm that can fill with beauty whatever time is necessary. A multilingual assembly will find the Lamb of God one of several times where it is appropriate and not that difficult to have the entire assembly learn a response that includes several languages.*

• *How many communion songs are enough? First, any communion song needs appropriate words and music. The assembly's words must be easy to learn by heart. Chants that are sung over and over again, compositions in which the assembly's part is strong and frequent but in dialogue with cantor or choir, psalms during which the assembly repeats an antiphon after each verse sung by choir or cantor are all appropriate forms. Six or eight well-known and well-loved communion songs may be enough for any assembly. One of these may be used for a whole season and then not sung again until that season returns.*

In learning to sing the communion rite, musicians and assembly learn about ritual music. Ritual music is music that is integral to the rite. It means singing the liturgy, not singing at the liturgy or singing during the liturgy. That is the goal—a rite that from the Lord's Prayer to the silence after communion is known and sung by heart.

The greatest challenge for the musician is finding pieces appropriate for the communion procession. Musicians should attend to the people who are actually processing. Are they singing their part? If, after giving a piece ample time, this is not happening, the piece is probably not a good communion song for this assembly.

The communion song should nearly always allow the choir to come forward at some point, with the assembly, to receive holy communion.

The Ministers of Communion

The minister of communion is one

- *who can stand before person after person and give full attention to each.*

- *who can look each person in the eyes and say, "The body of Christ," "The blood of Christ," without expanding those words (for example, "This is the body of Christ") so that those words stand in their wondrous ambiguity: the bread, the church, ourselves. (Augustine of Hippo said, "It is to what you yourselves are that you answer Amen. . . . Be a member of Christ's body so that your Amen may be authentic.")*

- *who can then be patient and not move until the Amen has been spoken.*

- *who can take bread and place it in the hands of the person, touching the communicant's hands without any haste at all, or who can, if the person chooses to receive on the tongue, do that with attention and reverence.*

- *who can with care and attention give the cup to a person.*

If there is a deacon assisting at the liturgy, see the notes for ministers of communion and those for acolytes. In addition, the deacon gives the invitation to exchange the kiss of peace. The rubrics say clearly that the deacon is to receive communion last.

Recommended resources for ministers of communion are *Guide for Ministers of Communion* by Victoria Tufano and *Video Guide for Ministers of Communion*. The latter offers good visual examples of the ministry as well as the testimony of communion ministers from two Chicago parishes. *The Communion Rite at Sunday Mass* has helpful insights throughout, but see especially pages 38–39, 50 and 97–100. Especially worthy of reflection is the quote from Robert Hovda on page 57.

Those who prepare ministers of communion for any reform of the parish practice should offer these veteran ministers the opportunity to study and discuss the entire communion rite, allowing them to share in at least some of the background work done by the core group. Most often ministers of communion will welcome these new efforts and will do all they can to be a full part of the renewal.

The following would be points to stress in discussing the communion rite in general with ministers of communion.

- *Communion ministers are members of the assembly who have offered their gifts to the rest of the assembly. But in every way possible, they should be model members of the assembly before, during and after the liturgy. This should be especially true during the Lord's Prayer and the kiss of peace.*

- *Each move the ministers make, each task they perform, is public and part of the church's celebration of the eucharist. Thus their manner in walking, standing, breaking the bread, pouring from the flagon, holding the plate or cup, matters greatly. The challenge is to manifest a great reverence for the Lord present in this assembly and in these gifts of bread and wine. That rules out any piety that calls attention to itself or to the minister. It rules out a casual manner that takes all depth away from these deeds. This reverence in posture and gesture does not mean a stiffness but a true liturgical piety that flows from ever greater gratitude for the gifts of God.*

  The person suited to this ministry is one who can translate that gratitude into posture, into the way in which the vessels are held, into the habit of looking each communicant in the eyes and saying to that person, "The body of Christ," "The blood of Christ," and truly listening to their Amen, then placing the bread in the hand or on the tongue with no haste, or the cup into the hands with no haste. Most parishes have one or more ministers who excel at this; sometimes other ministers can take inspiration simply from their example.

- *Bread and wine for the celebration of this eucharist are consecrated at this celebration. The tabernacle is not a storehouse holding consecrated bread for Sunday eucharist. The tabernacle holds consecrated bread for the communion of the sick and the dying, and for private devotion. Ministers should be alert to those rare occasions when they might be running out of bread and judge whether it will suffice to break the pieces smaller, to go to another station whose minister may be able to share, or—only as a last resort—to go to the tabernacle. The good sense in this will become clearer to all as the parish works on its celebration of the eucharistic prayer.*

- *The communion ministers do not receive communion last, rather than first, as a courtesy to the rest of the assembly (letting others go first). Rather, they do so to allow the communion rite to take place as intended, moving directly from the invitation to communion ("This is the lamb of God . . .") and the assembly's response, to the communion procession and the song of the assembly.*

- *Throughout their time in this ministry, communion ministers should hold themselves to the highest standard for the attention they give to each person who comes before them to receive the bread or the cup. For more on this, see especially the notes on pages 38–39 of* The Communion Rite at Sunday Mass *and the various comments and reflections made by ministers of communion in* Video Guide for Ministers of Communion *and* Say Amen! to What You Are.

If, in introducing various aspects of the renewal of the communion rite, the parish at large is invited to take part in study and discussions, ministers of communion can be asked to be leaders in small groups.

Ushers

In most parishes the ushers help people come forward pew by pew during the communion rite. Their ministry becomes even more important as a parish moves toward what can be called a "procession" more than a "line" for communion. This notion is explored in *The Communion Rite at Sunday Mass,* pages 60–77 ("A True Procession" and "Preparing a Procession"). This is not a simple matter of substituting a new set of directions to the ushers for an old set. They should have the opportunity to discuss and understand the notion of procession, and perhaps be involved in deciding how it can best be implemented given the floor plan and furniture of the church building.

The video *Say Amen! to What You Are* illustrates how a parish begins its communion procession during the Lamb of God, but more importantly it illustrates how that procession begins with those in the side seating. Pew by pew, people walk down the side aisles to the back and come in procession up the central aisle so that the feeling of movement permeates the whole assembly. The pages cited above in *The Communion Rite at Sunday Mass* explore how this approach can be used in other seating plans. Ushers will be crucial not only in making this work when it is new to the parish, but also in communicating understanding and enthusiasm for such a departure from the present "front row goes first" practice.

Other points for discussion and work with ushers include the following.

- *The ushers' role in the Lord's Prayer and the kiss of peace requires some reflection. Practices vary from parish to parish, but often ushers need encouragement to be model members of the assembly while still watching for any needs for assistance. They should model the parish posture for the Lord's Prayer wherever they are in the assembly. During the peace greeting, they can be especially attentive to those who may be isolated from the rest of the assembly.*

- *During preparation for communion, the ushers need to notice anyone who cannot come forward so that they can bring the minister of communion to these people, either before or after the procession.*

- *At the proper time (whether during the Lamb of God or immediately after the "Lord, I am not worthy . . .") the ushers begin the communion procession. For the first few months of a new form of communion procession, it helps for one usher to lead each line forward while another continues to move along the rows inviting people into the procession. The best way to order the procession usually generates a good conversation about what manner an usher should have. Just as with the communion ministers, there are usually a few ushers who show others what good ministry looks like (not too stiff, but also not the occasion for saying "Good morning" to everyone). Parishes are finding that all ushering tends to improve when women as well as men are involved.*

- *The ushers themselves come last in the procession. They should be encouraged to receive from the cup as well as the consecrated bread to model good communion practice for the rest of the assembly.*

Many questions about the ministry of ushers are explored in *Guide for Ushers and Greeters* by Lawrence Mick (available from LTP).

Acolytes

Though the ministry of the acolytes may change little as the communion rite is reformed, this can be the occasion for meeting to talk about what their job is in this part of the Mass and how best to do it. *Serve God with Gladness* by David Philippart (available from LTP) offers an overall approach to this ministry as well as excellent notes on the communion rite.

Acolytes, like all ministers, are members of the assembly first. They do what the assembly does. But they also give a special help to the presider and to other ministers so that the assembly's liturgy may be done fully, consciously, actively. Acolytes, like all the other ministers, should never do their tasks by rote. They need to understand the flow of the Sunday liturgy, how it moves from this to that, to be at home in it and thus really be able to help the assembly in its work.

Wherever the acolytes are during the eucharistic prayer and the communion rite, whether in full sight of the assembly or not, they should be models of full attention and participation. At the same time, we hope that young acolytes receive this example from the adult members of the assembly. Then, little by little, through experience and catechesis, their own sense of the beauty and importance of the liturgy will grow. For now, we can encourage acolytes to be attentive and to join the assembly in the posture of the Lord's Prayer, to chant it with everyone. Then, at the peace greeting, they should know how to greet each other and then go to the rest of the assembly, using both hands and looking people in the eye as they greet them.

When they return to their places, the acolytes bring the vessels for communion from the side table to the altar (unless this is the responsibility of the ministers of communion). They do this with care.

The acolytes respond with everyone to the invitation to communion, then throughout communion they join in singing the processional song. During the procession, it will probably be their responsibility to remove the book, the corporal and anything else from the altar. They receive communion in the order that is customary in the parish. If need be, they can help the ministers as the vessels are returned to the side table.

Along with the presider and the assembly, the acolytes are seated and silent after the communion procession. Usually one of them holds the book for the prayer after communion.

Sacristans

Increasingly, the ministry of the sacristan is being used and appreciated. Though many in the assembly will never know who the sacristan is, the parish's worship is immensely helped when this work is done well. Parishes should take this work seriously and have one sacristan for each weekend Mass. This minister becomes the one every other minister counts on week to week. When the sacristan's job is done well, it makes an immense difference to every other ministry, presider included. Two basic resources for the sacristan are *Guide for Sacristans* by Christina Neff and *The Sacristy Manual* by G. Thomas Ryan (both available from LTP). The latter has several sections that apply to the communion rite, especially "Wine and Vessels for Wine" (pages 108–13) and "Bread and Vessels for Bread" (pages 113–17).

The following are some main areas in this reform of the communion rite that will affect the sacristans.

- *In parishes that follow the "no hosts from the tabernacle" practice that has been part of the rubrics since 1970, the sacristan's responsibilities include preparing the proper amount of bread for each liturgy. This is determined by carefully tracked experience. It is not that difficult; in most parishes numbers do not vary greatly from week to week. Seasonal variations should be noted and kept on a calendar. If the bread is broken (all or most of it) before Mass, it is best kept in small containers holding a set number of pieces (50 generally works). That way, there never needs to be any last-minute counting. When the bread comes in larger pieces to be broken at the Mass (which is the preferred practice), sometimes the loaves are scored for a set number of pieces. Even so, only experience will tell the approximate number of pieces that a certain size loaf will yield. The benefit of the loaves, of course, is that pieces may be broken smaller and smaller if needed.*

- *The same care must go into the amount of wine. If the parish makes an effort to catechize about the cup, the number of people who regularly receive from the cup will grow. If there is only a tiny amount of wine in the cup, each communicant will take only a tiny sip. "Take and drink" is the invitation. The amount of wine in the cup should make it clear that a larger sip is acceptable. If that leads temporarily to consecrated wine that must be consumed by the ministers themselves at their communion or even after Mass, so be it. When ministers habitually offer only the smallest possible amount of wine, communicants will cease to receive from the cup. (And inevitably someone will claim that no one wants to receive from the cup.) So let the amount be ample, taking care that the consecrated wine remaining is consumed with reverence.*

- *The sacristan, through this whole period, could be involved in searching for better vessels if these are needed. The material in* The Sacristy Manual *may be of help here. Local artisans may be a good source for suitable vessels. See also* Basket, Basin, Plate and Cup *for good contemporary examples.*

- *Especially in large parishes, it may become the sacristan's task at Sunday Mass to serve the ministers of communion during the communion procession. When there are many communion stations, it is often best to leave some of the consecrated wine in the flagon on the altar. At some point, the sacristan may take this flagon and go to each of the stations to replenish the minister's cup. This may also be done with the consecrated bread. An additional minister of communion sometimes fulfills this task.*

- *If the renewal of the communion rite includes baking of the communion bread locally, the head sacristan will probably be the best person to oversee this ministry. A recipe for the bread can be found in either* The Sacristy Manual *(page 114) or* The Communion Rite at Sunday Mass *(page 78).*

- *Though the parish may have ministers of communion return after Mass and assist in washing the vessels, the sacristan will usually assist with this, making sure the vessels are put away or are in place for the next liturgy.*

Catechesis for the Assembly

All the resources cited in the notes above will be helpful in preparing catechesis for the assembly. Special attention should be given to the two pastoral letters (found in *Guide for Sunday*

Catechize the assembly

Mass and *Guide for the Assembly,* with its extensive study and discussion notes) and the homily-like texts presented in *Preaching about the Mass* and *Saving Signs, Wondrous Words.* Some resources (for example, *The Communion Rite at Sunday Mass* and *Clip Notes for Parish Bulletins,* also available from LTP) contain bulletin inserts that may be copied.

Prior to and permeating all efforts at catechesis with the assembly and with the whole parish is the enthusiasm and eagerness that should be generated by the pastor, the staff and the core group. This will catch on among the various persons in the ministries, and then among the whole assembly. This work is not drudgery or something that we have to grit our teeth and do. This is taking the next steps in the renewal of our church, the renewal mandated by Vatican II that has slowly been taking hold. It is a delight to be part of this.

The suggestions that follow emphasize the homily as a means of catechesis. In this year and in the years that follow, these notes are intended also for those who work in religious formation and education endeavors with both children and adults. Each year, beginning with this year on the communion rite, those who teach in the parish school, in religious education programs for children, in youth groups, and with adults should mine the resources suggested and the points stressed in the text of this book. Working together, the catechists should explore how they can let the catechesis done in the homily and parish bulletin enter into their own work from week to week.

The Homily

It is entirely in keeping with the directives for the homily that the homilist be free to base the preaching on the liturgy and its texts rather than on the scriptures alone. Thus, there can be a number of Sundays set aside in this period of work on the communion rite when the homilist will use every element of this rite as a resource for preaching: the bread, the wine, the vessels, the words, the chants, the procession, the kiss of peace, the Lord's Prayer, the silence, the human acts of eating and drinking. There is endless richness, and there are wonderful examples in the preaching of the ancient Fathers of the church.

These homilies will often be best prepared when the homilists spend time with several people, drawn perhaps from the core group and from the various ministries involved in the communion rite. This time can be spent simply discussing the power and beauty of the rites. The goal is not the outline of a homily but rather the enrichment of the homilist. Later, the homilist may want to reconvene this group and test with them the direction taken with the homily, allowing time for further work after their comments.

Such homilies are not intended as "here's what we're going to do" time. That can come in other forms: the bulletin, sessions after Mass, even—on a few Sundays—a short presentation just before Sunday Mass. The homily is still a homily. Because the homilist has been challenged to ponder and explore the communion rite, the homily can share what the homilist now sees and challenge all to do their own exploring.

That is not to say that the homilist doesn't touch on what the parish practice will soon be, or has recently become. The posture for the Lord's Prayer, the litany form of the Lamb of God, drinking from the cup, procession rather than line are all the stuff of the homily. But the homily is about more than how to do something. It is far more about what becomes of us (the church) when we are formed by good liturgical practice. The homily is one person's best effort to reflect on how doing these things will form us as Christians, form us for life. Thus the homilist explores not so much "what does it mean to raise our arms and pray the Lord's Prayer," but rather "who and whose and what are we who pray with our arms raised this way?"

Clearly there are times in the liturgical year that lend themselves to such preaching (for example, the feast of the Body and Blood of Christ, the five Sundays in Year B when John chapter 6 is read, and the whole Easter season any year), but the parish should not feel restricted to these. The actual timing of the introduction of the small and large changes in present practice of the communion rite is best left to local judgment. Common sense suggests that Advent, Christmas season and Lent are probably not good times because they have their own needs. The Easter season does also, but its very nature lends itself well to any effort to build up the church through stronger Sunday liturgy. The summer and the fall also, in many parishes, are excellent for both catechesis and the introduction of new practices.

What is begun this year should become a permanent element in the parish's approach to preaching: allowing the deeds, words, objects and songs of the liturgy to be a constant and vital element of what the homilist considers when preparing to preach. For more on this approach to preaching, see Edward Foley's *Preaching Basics* (available from LTP), especially the section "The Liturgical Bible," pages 13–14.

Catechesis and the Communion Procession: Some Specifics

Procession is not a bad way to think about our Sunday liturgy. The assembly does its gathering, which is a procession that concludes when some of the ministers take their places. We are on the move again as we near the time to proclaim the gospel. Catechumens process out after their dismissal. Then there is a procession centering on money, bread and wine: We are coming to the table. The communion procession continues this and, in fact, is a kind of climax. After the dismissal, another procession begins with the ministers and concludes with the whole assembly going out.

Sunday liturgy is not sedentary business. We are on the move. But the movement of the whole assembly to the banquet, the movement of all those "called to his supper," is surely the procession when we can sense (see, hear, experience in our own bodies) how we are the church at worship. Most Catholics are ready to hear and accept this. Some grew up thinking that intense personal prayer is the only dimension of holy communion. This is only *one* dimension, and it can only be enhanced by the parish's regular practice of a sacred and prayerful procession in which the ecclesial piety flourishes and, in fact, is personal. It helps greatly if the renewed communion rite takes seriously the regular practice of silence after communion, when all—ministers included—simply sit (or kneel if some wish) and pray silently.

Far more Catholics, perhaps, have grown up not quite knowing what is or should be intense about holy communion. For them, good catechesis in preaching and other ways can open up the rite as never before.

Before looking at a few specifics, it must be said that catechesis will do nothing if the parish is not ready to implement well what is being discussed and explained. Steady experience over several months is what will bring forth delight in at last being able to participate in liturgy fully, consciously, actively. Then we have begun to put on a liturgical piety.

In the course of catechesis with the assembly, in whatever forms that takes, keep in mind these points about the communion procession that should be pondered, held up for attention, applied. Remember that this catechesis is never a matter of saying, "Okay, from now on I want to see you all with your hands folded in that communion procession." Rather, it is about calling people to ponder with the homilist what we believe about our holy communion, about the tradition in which we walk, about how we take responsibility to manifest the mystery and hand on the tradition. That is done far more in posture and in participation than it is in theological words separated from practice. The theologian-homilist is there to raise up the connections that need to be made between life and liturgy. These include a number of things, including those below.

- *Posture in the procession. How do we walk in this procession? There is no imposing a single posture on those coming to holy communion. Yet the communal nature of what we do would suggest that it is at least permissible to take a specific posture. That is, it is permitted to walk with hands folded or to walk forward to the table in a posture of readiness, hands already made into what the church has called a "throne" for the eucharistic Lord, one hand cupped inside the other, and then both hands extended. It is presumed that the songs used at communion never require that the assembly use a book, so there is not a question of book or participation aid in people's hands in the procession (or even when they are not in the procession).*

  Regarding the "throne" we make with our open hands and hold forth to receive the food and drink, the text from Augustine should be quoted even more often: "What does it mean to stretch out one's hand, knowing that one must provide the same kind of meal oneself? As Christ laid down his life for us, so we are in our turn to lay down our lives for our brothers and sisters." Now that is preaching from the liturgy! And all of that is there in the ritual posture and gesture: stretching out the hands, the hunger and the thirst, the yearning to be fed and to taste and to see. If communion is, by definition, about solidarity, then here in my outstretched hands is my solidarity not only with the church but with the hungry, with the poor, with humankind and with all creatures who are daily hungry, daily in need of food and drink. The homilist, in fact, should be exhorting us all to cherish these procession times on Sundays when we can put our empty hands out and be who we truly are, who we are learning to be.

  And after receiving holy communion, what is the posture for the rest of the procession, the return to one's place? Perhaps this is the time to ask: Why does it look so casual? Or so private? Is folding hands an option here?

- *Song in the procession. We process singing. Coming to and from the table, to and from the sacred banquet, we sing, letting the song permeate our minds and also our steps, our rhythm of movement. A refrain that punctuates the verses sung by cantor or choir, or a piece that is repeated over and over (as many Taizé pieces are)—a selection of these make up a repertoire that the whole assembly, over the course of a year, comes to know and love.*

But the assembly needs to be asked sometimes by the homilist to ponder the texts as well as the melody of the parish's communion songs. What is their poetry bringing forward? How does one absorb it, make it part of life? Where else in life might these words and tunes show up? Sometimes the assembly needs to be encouraged, even exhorted: If you leave the singing to others, you abandon this deed of holy communion, you diminish the church in its service to the Lord. The song is not something to pass the time, it is the liturgy.

- *Receiving the bread and cup. Many in the assembly will welcome a time to reflect with the homilist on the manner of receiving. There is, of course, no one right way to do it. But there are many ways that fail to convey reverence or the ecclesial dimensions of this act. Some people have grown casual if not sloppy. Others have become mechanical; still others seem unaware that the whole church is in this sacred banquet.*

  Periodically we need to be challenged: Do you stand straight with your hands extended (or folded if you receive on your tongue) before the minister of communion and listen to what is being said, "The body of Christ," "The blood of Christ"? Do you continue to look at the minister as you proclaim "Amen!" to this? Do you remain for that few seconds, facing the minister, gazing at the hands and the bread, until the bread has been placed in your hand and the minister's hand is removed from yours? Do you step aside and pause a moment as you bring the consecrated bread to your mouth? Do you take the cup firmly with both hands from the minister and bring it to your lips, then place the cup just as firmly back into the hands of the minister? These questions need to be posed more than once in a lifetime!

  These questions are about more than good practice. They are about the fundamental Christian deed, our feeding on the body and blood of the Lord. The way we do this—as a church!—does far more than all our textbooks and cate-chisms to convey what it is that we baptized people believe to be the foundation of God's reign proclaimed by Jesus: "The reign of God is like . . ." So we must be called again and again to be attentive to what we do, and so to allow the power of this deed to shape us, little by little, through the Sundays of our lives.

- *The fast. The one-hour fast before holy communion is a token fast, not a real one. The problem is that as a token it gets for-gotten, loses its place in the tradition. Should it? Part of preaching on our holy communion should call us to be atten-tive to this fast, to reflect on the tradition and how it might become something important in our community now. The fast before communion is, at least in part, about anticipation. It is like the fast of Good Friday and Holy Saturday before the Vigil, when we are to be so full of what is to happen, so full of excitement, that the stomach forgets to complain. We get hungry for God's word and hungry for the body and blood of the Lord. We come to church hungry. We need to come to church hungry, need to be reminded in our bodies of impor-tant things.*

  For Americans this fast might well be many-dimensioned. We clear the eyes, the ears, the senses. Does it really work to read the newspaper or watch TV or listen to the radio before Mass on Sunday? This discussion is not just about the communion rite; it can come up again throughout the reform of parish Sunday liturgy because it points toward an indis-pensable part of our liturgy: the assembly—as much as the cantor, as much as the homilist, as much as the presider— must come prepared for what is to be done.

- *The cup. "Take this, all of you, and drink it." Little by little, we are getting there. But the corner yet to be turned in most parishes is to know that the cup is not something extra, some-thing eccentric. Receiving holy communion under both species is the norm, the fullness of sacrament that we Catholics are forever seeking. Catechesis and preaching must address this positively, as the restoration of an ancient fullness. It must be part of preparation for first eucharist, part of all teaching in the parish school and religious education program about the Mass. Without this, it is hard to speak of full participation. As people pass by the cup, we feel the long-lasting affects of a minimalism that said a few drops of water were enough to baptize, that one seldom needed to come to holy communion. And we feel also a certain cultural refusal: In this society people do not drink from a common vessel. But to that refusal we must respond, "Except here!"*

The deed of drinking from a common vessel manifests and forms how the reign of God is to be. We need to recognize something simple: We thirst. And to come to the cup is to acknowledge our thirst and to know that our thirst is satisfied only in this cup that is Christ's blood poured out for us. We need to reflect on the fact that we use wine—not water, not juice, but wine—which carries all sorts of ambiguous baggage, and is so different from bread in meaning. Those who address this should attend especially to the wisdom of parishioners in the video Say Amen! to What You Are, *and perhaps to the celebration of the vine and cup in Photina Rech's* Wine and Bread *(available from LTP), a poetic exploration of these two foods in scripture and tradition.*

- *Posture of the assembly. Nowhere do the rubrics call for the assembly to kneel during any part of the communion rite. It is traditional in the United States to do so, but the renewal of this part of the liturgy challenges this practice. Catechesis and preaching need to address this issue of posture, calling attention to the way kneeling or sitting before or after communion can completely undo the meaning of what is taking place at the sacred banquet. It is the church that is called to the Lord's supper, and we come as members of the church.*

This cannot be simply a matter of "We ask you to remain standing." There must be an attentive standing, a participatory standing, a singing standing, a working standing. The spirituality here is the solidarity of the body of Christ, the fullness of holy communion manifest in our all-so-human assembly. For some, kneeling will continue to be a necessity. Others need to sit down for various reasons. The goal is simply that the norm in our assemblies is standing together, in communion, until everyone has received communion and we

Implement the changes

List the particular changes you will undertake.	Beginning date	Check-up date

can all sit down together, the song completed, to keep silent and still. That silent, seated time after communion ought to be established practice when the transition to standing during communion is made.

Throughout this year's catechesis, in preaching and by other means, and in the years that follow, a crucial factor is attitude. This renewal is not about window dressing, not about fussiness, and not about disturbing people. It is about the church that we can be, the church that pours itself out each Sunday in celebrating fully the liturgy renewed by Vatican II, the liturgy that is strong enough to continue forming us life-long in the gospel. That can lead to talk about details—the cup, the posture after communion—because it is in these details that we will achieve the habit of participation. But preachers and teachers must themselves be so imbued with liturgy and the hunger for it that they draw others after them. That is exactly what was intended in the mandate in article 14 of the *Constitution on the Sacred Liturgy.*

∽ **Resources** to Gather for Year Three

All of these resources are available from Liturgy Training Publications: 1-800-933-1800. Those marked with an asterisk (*) can be found in the anthology *The Liturgy Documents, Volume One.*

Roman Documents

General Instruction of the Roman Missal*

U.S. Documents

Pastoral Letter of Cardinal Roger Mahony *Gather Faithfully Together* (also available as *Guide for Sunday Mass,* in English and Spanish)

Pastoral Letter of Cardinal Joseph Bernardin *Our Communion, Our Peace, Our Promise* (also available as *Guide for the Assembly,* in English and Spanish)

Books

Richard McCarron, *The Eucharistic Prayer at Sunday Mass*

Nathan Mitchell and John Leonard, *The Posture of the Assembly during the Eucharistic Prayer*

Gabe Huck, *Preaching about the Mass*

David Philippart, *Saving Signs, Wondrous Words*

Videos

Video Guide to Gather Faithfully Together

Lift Up Your Hearts: The Eucharistic Prayer (part four of *The Sunday Mass Series)*

Year Three

The Eucharistic Prayer

Once the communion rite begins to be the "by heart" work of the assembly, the need for full celebration of the eucharistic prayer will be obvious. The challenges here are different. This part of the liturgy often looks like this:

- *The time for the preparation of the gifts is neither reflective nor preparatory.*

- *The eucharistic prayer has no clear beginning.*

- *Whatever attention the assembly has summoned for the preface is lost after the Holy, Holy.*

- *The rest of the eucharistic prayer is, for most of the assembly, an unremarkable blur, the end of which (though few would make a distinction) is the Lord's Prayer.*

- *When asked about what happens between the Holy, Holy and the Lord's Prayer, most people are hard-pressed to say anything beyond "the consecration."*

That is not the situation in all parishes, but it shouldn't be the situation in any parish. The *General Instruction of the Roman Missal* states:

Now the center and summit of the entire celebration begins: the eucharistic prayer, a prayer of thanksgiving and sanctification. The priest invites the people to lift up their hearts to the Lord in prayer and thanks; he unites them with himself in the prayer he addresses in their name to the Father through Jesus Christ. The meaning of the prayer is that the entire congregation joins itself to Christ in acknowledging the great things God has done and in offering the sacrifice. (#54)

Toward such a praying, the basic approach used in Year Two is applied to the renewal of the eucharistic prayer, along with the preparation of the gifts that precedes it, in Year Three:

• *Using some of the resources listed below (and on page 68), and using this chapter itself as a starting point, the core group explores the rite: the history and current shape of the eucharistic prayer, the ministries involved, the present practice, other possibilities. An initial session may take an introductory look at the rite as a whole from each of these perspectives. Following sessions may then delve more thoroughly into this central prayer of the church. An important element in these discussions will be mystagogy: discovering how people can speak from their own experience about the mystery we celebrate. Along the way, only this chapter itself need be read by all. Other reading can be divided: different people read from different resources and then report to the whole group. The group should gather for discussion at least once a month.*

• *These discussions will unfold the strengths and weaknesses of the present practice. Notes of key observations should be made along the way. Experiences should be heard and pondered. Throughout there should be a concerted effort to discover and discuss what the church intends by this prayer and how week-by-week parish practice might best express this. We are on the way to asking: Can we envision the best celebration of the eucharistic prayer and the steps we must take to get there? It may work best to focus on the eucharistic prayer, deliberately delaying discussion of the preparation of the gifts until later. The group will answer the following questions about the eucharistic prayer: How and by whom are the texts for the preface and the eucharistic prayer chosen for a given season or Sunday? How are presiders to lead this prayer? What is the role of the cantor? How will we convey to ourselves and to the assembly the kind of energy and attention we are to pour into this prayer? How do we see for ourselves and for the assembly the implications of eucharistic praying? Those involved are likely to face again and again the fact that the renewal of the liturgy of the eucharistic prayer (unlike the communion rite) depends greatly on presiders who strive to grasp both the centrality of the prayer and the essential qualities of one who leads it.*

- *Explore resources and occasions for the broader catechesis of the assembly. How can a significant portion of the assembly be drawn into the discussion, asked to read and ponder, and addressed in the homily? These discussions should always consider the seasons and the lectionary as they plan for catechesis and preaching. What season or what section of Ordinary Time will be appropriate for homilies and written materials to address the importance of the eucharistic prayer in the life of this parish? Along with this, how will the ministries involved in the preparation rite and the eucharistic prayer be addressed: acolytes, ushers, cantors and presiders?*

- *After preparation and catechesis, how will implementation take place: all at once or one element at a time? What continuing catechesis will be offered?*

- *Finally, great attention is needed as implementation begins. Patience and firmness might be the best qualities to seek here. It will take many Sundays before the sought-after qualities take hold. Along the way, some form of evaluation and thoughtful critique is essential.*

Resources

Read and study
All would benefit from viewing together *Lift Up Your Hearts: The Eucharistic Prayer* (part four of *The Sunday Mass Series)*, which records the praying of the eucharistic prayer at St. Peter Church in Cleveland, Ohio, and includes comments by members of the assembly. This video is a witness to the formative work of the eucharistic prayer when catechesis and ritual allow all to participate fully. While the physical setting and size of the assembly may be quite different from what this parish experiences, the attention and devotion of the assembly, along with their eloquence in speaking of the eucharistic prayer, will bridge these gaps.

The following sections of resources listed in Year One are also essential to this year's discussions and preparations.

Assigned to:	*The Eucharistic Prayer at Sunday Mass* by Richard McCarron
_____ _____ _____	This book is the basic resource for this entire year. At least one member of the group needs to have a thorough knowledge of it, though the entire group may be asked to read some sections. Texts from this book constitute the general shape of the study outlined below.

Assigned to:	*General Instruction of the Roman Missal*, 49–55, 100–10
_____ _____ _____	*Gather Faithfully Together (Guide for Sunday Mass)*, 63–68, 160–63
	Video Guide to Gather Faithfully Together Review and pay close attention to the section of the eucharistic prayer that is recorded.
	Our Communion, Our Peace, Our Promise (Guide for the Assembly), 52–64

Short sections of the following two books, first used in Year Two, are also helpful. They can be read together:

Preaching about the Mass, "The Liturgy of the Eucharist I," pages 42–50 *Saving Signs, Wondrous Words,* "We Bring You These Gifts," pages 28–30; "Calling to Mind and Ready to Greet Him," pages 31–34; "Let Your Spirit Come upon These Gifts," pages 35–37; "Through Human Hands," pages 38–40	**Assigned to:** _____ _____ _____

In addition, the following will be helpful:

The Posture of the Assembly during the Eucharistic Prayer by Nathan Mitchell and John Leonard This is a brief but thorough look at the tradition.	**Assigned to:** _____ _____ _____

Remember, the above readings can be divided up among the members of the core group, with those who do the reading reporting to the rest during the course of the discussions. But all members of the core group should read the rest of this chapter.

The Preparation of the Gifts and the Eucharistic Prayer: An Overview

When the intercessions have ended, the entire assembly relaxes a bit. The hard work of listening and interceding is finished. The hard work of praise and thanksgiving is ahead. In between, it is fairly quiet. Reverently, but without calling any particular attention to themselves, acolytes place cup and

Plan changes

book on the altar. Then, in some order that is established and works well, the gifts for the church and the poor are gathered by ministers or brought forward by the assembly. This is an informal but important time when one important sign of each baptized person's responsibility is made. Real bread and ample wine, in beautiful containers that point not to themselves but to what they hold, are brought reverently to the altar. The cup is filled with wine, and there are quiet prayers that accompany the preparation of both cup and bread, as well as the washing of the hands. There may be silence or music or song, but nothing to give the impression that anything other than preparation is taking place. Finally, when all is ready, the presider quietly proclaims the prayer over the gifts to which all respond, "Amen." On the table now are the bread on its plate, the wine in its cup and in whatever other vessel is needed to have enough for all, and the book. (A helpful discussion of the preparation of the gifts, including, options for parish practice, can be found in *The Eucharistic Prayer at Sunday Mass*, pages 118–27.)

The assembly is standing. No other moment of the Sunday liturgy calls for presider and assembly to be both in dialogue and, at the same time, to be one. At no other moment does it make such sense that the presider be "held" by the assembly, and that the assembly have a sense of themselves as church: hearing and seeing one another around the bread and wine placed on their altar, acclaiming the mystery here proclaimed and realized. Important as the words that the presider will pronounce are, we are a people of sight, absorbing more from what we see than from what we hear. Thus it matters immensely that the assembly throughout the prayer can see the church assembled, can see the leader of the prayer, and can even see the table and the bread and the wine. It matters then that this bread and this wine themselves proclaim to our sight their goodness, their beauty, their simplicity. In some places, especially where the building is long and narrow, it may be good practice for many in the assembly to come forward to surround the altar on all sides except the side that remains open to those who choose to stay put.

So there is need here—between the "Amen" to the prayer over the gifts and the address, "The Lord be with you"—for the climate in the room to change. Taking some time for it helps that.

After this usual greeting and response ("And also with you"), the first formal words at the table are spoken in our ancient dialogue: "Lift up your hearts!" That *sursum corda*—"hearts on high!"—is the church's summons, used since the first centuries of our existence, to do what baptized people do on the Lord's Day. This is a summons to begin the most intense time of the Mass, a time when all of us who are so invited are to exercise the rights and the duties of the baptized, to do so in our muscles and our voices, to do so with sound and posture and gesture. Thus our whole lives are to be taken up in the life and prayer of this body of Christ, this church.

The dialogue is sung, chanted, even if on a single note. Thus the prayer is lifted up from the speaking voice. Everyone knows the dialogue and can feel that it is a call to attend (that is, to be fully alert, attentive, "present" in every sense). The back-and-forth does what it says: All are lifted up. These are the basic words of Christian vocabulary: "We lift them up to the Lord" to "give thanks and praise." These are crucial words: This dialogue has defined us since the first centuries of Christianity. In these words begin any theology, any spirituality. Without them, any theology, any spirituality, will be lacking, will fail to comprehend the most basic proclamation of the baptized.

Then the one presiding—and it is in these moments that the art of presiding is exercised—now energized by the assembly's acclamation, continues. The words chanted flow out of the dialogue and flow toward the acclamatory hymn of the Holy, Holy.

"Flow" is the key notion. One act does not end with some words about joining "with the angels." Rather, the Holy, Holy nearly overlaps the presider's conclusion (no instrumental introduction is necessary, and in some cases, no instruments at all are necessary) as all become a part of the song.

The singing of the Holy, Holy flows back into the chanted proclamation of the presider. The unity of the eucharistic prayer is witnessed by the elevated voice from beginning to end. Whichever eucharistic prayer is being prayed, the presider's attention to the text calls forth the assembly's attention. That is not to say the text is merely on the page: It is certainly there on the page, but the presider knows it so well that the prayer is not an exercise in reading, but in proclaiming a lengthy, many-faceted prayer to the Father, a prayer whose structure and texture the presider knows, in the most urgent sense, by heart.

Whether the assembly breaks into this text only three times (the Holy, Holy, the memorial acclamation, the Amen) or many times (as in Eucharistic Prayer II for Masses with Children), there should never be a sense that this is a long prayer in which the leader stops once in a while for a short song. On the contrary, the sense, built by years of Sunday praying this way, is to be: Here is the root of all Christian praying, the back-and-forth of proclamation and acclamation in which the whole church makes eucharist and eucharist makes the whole church!

We cannot pretend now to know what this doing of the eucharistic prayer by presider and assembly really is. We are too new to it. It needs time to become the norm, the right and duty of the baptized. But we do know that it is a school of praise and thanksgiving in which the many deeds of God may be named, and a few deeds—those that are at the heart of what we Christians remember—are always named. This deepest Christian memory is the passion and death and resurrection of our Lord Jesus Christ, and in remembering this the presider asks that the Holy Spirit come upon the gifts of bread and wine "to make them holy so that they may become for us the body and blood of our Lord Jesus Christ."

A basic telling of the paschal deed is always proclaimed: "On the night he was betrayed . . ." This "institution narrative" does not drop out of the prayer as if it were a story to reenact—the words are addressed to God, not the assembly. This remembering of the passion, death and resurrection of the Lord is proclaimed as a prayer (it is prayer!). The assembly's acclamation proclaims in various ways the mystery of faith; by this acclamation we are witnesses to the vitality of that paschal mystery.

When this prayer is done regularly with the full, conscious and active participation of the assembly, its dominant tone is praise and thanksgiving, not adoration. The eucharistic prayer has little if anything of the focus on adoration that characterized later devotions to the blessed sacrament (which arose when the faithful were allowed little if any active participation in the eucharistic prayer), such as the rite of benediction. We simply need to recognize that, rejoice in the breadth and variety of our ritual system, and go on to let the eucharistic prayer be the eucharistic prayer.

In the structure of the prayer, our remembering—after it prompts our praise and thanksgiving—dwells in detail on the deeds and words of Jesus at the Last Supper, and leads us then to offer to the Father the sacrifice that Christ is for us. It then turns toward the living and the dead, the church and the saints. All of this we bring before the Father, proclaiming finally that it is through and with and in Christ, in the unity of the Holy Spirit, that all honor and glory belong to God.

Whether or not the assembly has acclaimed aloud or silently during this latter part of the prayer, every acclamation is summed up in the Great Amen. The holy bread and cup are lifted high, in a gesture proclaiming that the breadth and depth and height of all we have said and who we are is here in mystery, in the gift of God and the work of human hands.

What Needs Attention?

Plan changes

That is the eucharistic prayer. It is intense, routine in the best sense and exhausting. It is anything but a time-out while the presider monopolizes the liturgy; on the contrary it is the time when the assembly rises to great attention and participation. Getting to that point requires time spent on many questions, leading to a number of shared assumptions among those responsible for preparing the liturgy. Then comes careful preparation of the ministers and energetic catechesis of the assembly. What follows is a look at some of the matters with which the core group, then the ministers and others, must deal during this year. Together with the description of the eucharistic prayer just given and matters raised by the other resources recommended, the following areas call for consideration and resolution in parish practice.

The Choice of Preface and Prayer

Dozens of texts for the preface and, at present, ten texts for the eucharistic prayer are given in the sacramentary. The choice of preface is limited by the season (or feast) or, in some cases, by the choice of the eucharistic prayer itself. But even so, most Sundays offer more than one possibility. *The Eucharistic Prayer at Sunday Mass* (pages 63–68) provides an excellent overview of the eucharistic prayers.

For both preface and eucharistic prayer, these things matter:

- *The assembly is respected; thus the choice is made well in advance. The presider does not decide on the spot. The preface should be appropriate to the Sunday (echoing, perhaps, an element of the scripture during Ordinary Time) but also rhetorically strong (some prefaces are much more so than others). The eucharistic prayer should be chosen for a season or a long segment of Ordinary Time, not for a single week. Thus, for example, Eucharistic Prayer for Reconciliation I might be chosen for use on all the Sundays of Lent, year after year. This seasonal consistency builds familiarity with these foundational words of Catholic prayer.*

- *Someone involved in the preparation of the liturgy needs to know the prefaces well. Whether this is the presider or someone else, well ahead of any season and well ahead of the various segments of Ordinary Time, this person posts the choices. This allows presiders to rehearse even familiar words, and it allows musicians involved in the music of the prayer to prepare for acclamations, including the Holy, Holy.*

- *The eucharistic prayer will not become vital by being long, but some length is necessary simply to establish its place within the whole liturgy. Eucharistic Prayer II is probably too brief to allow for the rhythm of frequent acclamation, making it a fine choice perhaps for weekdays, but not for Sunday. The length of Eucharistic Prayer III and of the two Eucharistic Prayers for Reconciliation seem from experience to be closest to ideal, especially when chanted by the presider. The addition of assembly acclamations does not make them too lengthy.*

  Eucharistic Prayers I and IV are longer without, perhaps, the stronger rhetoric needed to sustain that length. Parishes often seem to designate one or the other of these two prayers for some major feast days within each year. If this practice is judged a good one in the local situation, then it will need to be consistent from year to year, and each time the presider will have to prepare well to proclaim in speech or chant these long and less familiar texts.

- *One important reason that a parish establishes a schedule for preface and eucharistic prayer is to allow the homilist to draw from these texts. If it is known that all through the Easter season, at every liturgy of every Sunday, Eucharistic Prayer III will be prayed, and the proper preface for each Sunday is listed, then these texts can go alongside the scriptures as homilists prepare. Only thus can the whole assembly gradually ponder these crucial and often beautiful texts. This is what mystagogy means in preaching: The homilist draws on the ritual vocabulary of the liturgy in order to open up both the richness of that vocabulary and its importance to daily life.*

There is another strong argument for returning to the same texts for the same season year after year. In doing so, as with hymns and other music, the parish little by little achieves a sense of being at home in each of the seasons. Far from meaningless repetition, this frees people to go deeper and deeper into the mystery.

How the Prayer Is Proclaimed

Train the ministers

The eucharistic prayer, from the invitation to lift up our hearts until the Great Amen, is public prayer.

First, it is prayer. Once the initial dialogue ends, all that is chanted by the presider is the church's voice addressed to the Father, repeating Sunday by Sunday the strongest words we have to express our most basic stance as those baptized in Christ. It is prayer; it is not a homily, not a creed, not an exhortation, not an exercise in drama.

But this prayer has many moments. Presiders, with the help of others, should explore the various modes this prayer takes as it unfolds: thanksgiving; epiclesis (calling the Holy Spirit to sanctify the gifts of bread and wine, and with this to transform us); anamnesis (or memorial—we remember God's actions, but especially the passion and death and resurrection of Jesus) and offering; intercession; doxology. (See Richard McCarron's discussion of these moments in *The Eucharistic Prayer at Sunday Mass*, pages 51–62.)

All of these elements constitute prayer addressed to the Father. All have great importance, and together they form a single prayer rather than a random arrangement of many individual prayers.

Second, the prayer is public, not in the sense that it is prayed in front of others, but in the sense that it is the prayer of this church assembled. Nothing should distract from that; nothing should lead us to think that the whole prayer or any part of it, like the quiet prayer the presider says just before taking holy communion, is a personal and private prayer.

Understanding and achieving a proper manner for praying public prayers, then, is part of the work of this year. Apart from his voice, the presider's posture, relationship to the assembly, to the altar and to the book are all vital. All of these must be considered. (The examples given in the videos *Lift Up Your Hearts, The Roman Catholic Mass Today* and *Video Guide to Gather Faithfully Together* may be of some help here, though every place and assembly will have its own demands.)

When a parish has more than one presider, it must struggle with the question of what is to be consistent among them all (for example, how they express in their posture and with their hands what the rubrics prescribe) and what will vary. It is a delicate matter to work out what is obligatory in leading this prayer and where there is some room for individual expression. In proclaiming the eucharistic prayer, a presider is never to manifest a piety that is not the piety of this prayer. This privatizing happens, for example, when a presider exaggerates the gesture or the length of the lifting of the host or the cup within the institution narrative, or when a presider is casual or mechanical in style. Distracting or stagy mannerisms during the eucharistic prayer turn the assembly into an audience, watching passively (or losing interest) at the very moments the presider's every action should be eliciting the assembly's highest attention.

As far as the voice itself is concerned, the presider is addressing God. Only in the opening dialogue and in the invitation to the memorial acclamation ("Let us proclaim the mystery of faith") is the assembly addressed. Voice (and eyes) must show this. The assembly is to pray with, not be entertained or bored or inspired by, the presider. This requires that presiders have a great familiarity with the texts of the prefaces and eucharistic prayers so that they are freed, to the greatest extent possible, from the page. It requires that the presider respect and hold in awe these texts so that they are not lightly uttered.

Chant can give to the eucharistic prayer what public prayer requires. This need not be elaborate; even a single tone for the entire prayer serves to lift up the eucharistic prayer as central to our liturgy. It helps if the entire prayer is chanted and not just some parts; this communicates the unity of the prayer. When the prayer is chanted, it is difficult to go too fast, difficult to go too slow, and difficult to impose one's own theology or piety or desire for dramatic speaking on the prayer. Chant makes the sung acclamations of the assembly seem at home within the prayer, not at all an interruption for song. Also, chant helps the words to be clear and draws attention to the words and not to the one speaking them.

Acclamations

Train the ministers

The assembly's part of the eucharistic prayer is not limited to a bodily and aural attentiveness. This is a prayer of proclamation and acclamation. The assembly's acclamations (even if limited to the Holy, Holy, memorial acclamation and Great Amen) are part of the prayer, not short time-outs from prayer. The acclamations are to flow from and into the proclamation of the presider.

The sense of an acclamation is in the verb "to acclaim." We have heard something said in the context of our gathering around our altar-table with the bread and wine placed upon that table, and we acclaim all of this. Even the lengthy Holy, Holy partakes of this acclamatory nature: "Hosanna, hosanna in the highest!" This song within the eucharistic prayer is not like and should not sound like our singing of processional music at entrance or communion, not like our litanies of Kyrie or Lamb of God, with a litany's contemplative or intensifying repetition, not like the psalm and its refrain after the first reading.

These words are like the Alleluia, the liturgy's other acclamation. In *Music in Catholic Worship* they are called "shouts of joy which arise from the whole assembly as forceful and meaningful assents to God's word and action" (#53). That is a good measure for the qualities to seek in any acclamations, whose music the assembly is to learn by heart. In this connection we note that the rubrics suggest that the Alleluia never be spoken. If it cannot for some reason be sung, it is omitted altogether. No similar rubric exists for these acclamations within the eucharistic prayer, but the logic is the same—not to acclaim in song would be disastrous.

It is not as important that everyone know the difference between a litany and an acclamation, but it is very important that anyone who is regularly part of the assembly know melodies by heart to sing these acclamations. These are not choir pieces. They are not cantor-and-assembly pieces once they are known by heart. They should not need instrumental introductions that break the flow of proclamation and acclamation. Each assembly, each parish even, needs only one of these tunes that can be sung every Sunday at every liturgy, because what Sundays have in common far outweighs what distinguishes them (for example, being in Lent or in the Easter season). But most assemblies can learn by heart a few tunes for acclamations: one or two for Ordinary Time, two or three that carry the sense of the particular seasons. When additional acclamations are part of praying the eucharistic prayer, these short lines should be sung with tunes derived from the Holy, Holy, memorial acclamation and Amen.

The Eucharistic Prayer at Sunday Mass asks three questions about the melodies for singing the acclamations (see the discussion in that book, pages 92–100):

- *Does the music serve for proclaiming this prayer? The goal is to find music that is wedded to text, a unity that is experienced in the singing.*

- *Does the music engage the assembly in such a way that the prayer is experienced as an action of the gathered assembly?*

- *Does the music contribute to a sense of the prayer as a unified whole?*

These questions point us toward our experience of various tunes and how they are used in order to measure their usefulness in the liturgy. When we decide as a parish that one year from now the eucharistic prayer will be the heart and soul of our life together, then we have to face the search for just a few good melodies for acclamations, strong enough to endure.

Train the ministers

The Altar, the Bread and the Wine

In the midst of the assembly is its altar. *Environment and Art in Catholic Worship* says this:

> *The altar, the holy table, should be the most noble, the most beautifully designed and constructed table the community can provide. It is the common table of the assembly, a symbol of the Lord, at which the presiding minister stands and upon which are placed the bread and wine and their vessels and the book. It is holy and sacred to this assembly's action and sharing, so it is never used as a table of convenience or as a resting place for papers, notes, cruets, or anything else. It stands free, approachable from every side, capable of being encircled. It is desirable that candles, cross, any flowers or other decoration in the area should not be so close to the altar as to constitute impediments to anyone's approach or movement around the common table.*
>
> *The altar is designed and constructed for the action of a community and the functioning of a single priest—not for concelebrants. The holy table, therefore, should not be elongated, but square or slightly rectangular, an attractive, impressive, dignified, noble table, constructed with solid and beautiful materials, in pure and simple proportions. (#71–72)*

Note all of the characteristics of an altar from those two paragraphs, and use them to evaluate the altar of the parish. No altar will have all of these qualities, but this evaluation becomes an occasion to discuss this most central but often neglected symbol within our church. If the altar does have all those qualities, then this may be the year to consider how the altar is clothed. In some places, this may be the year to consider where the altar is placed: Is it freestanding? Is it approachable from every side? Can it be encircled? During this year, there might be an occasion when all, entering in procession, would kiss the altar as the presider does at the beginning and end of the liturgy.

Is there a habit of placing on the altar anything other than the vessels of bread and wine and the book? How can this habit be ended? When the vessels and book are placed on the altar, is the book centered from left to right and on the edge toward the presider, with the vessels then toward the assembly? This allows the vessels to be central. Note that the additional plates, cups and purificators for holy communion are not brought forward until the breaking of the bread. If the acoustics of the room or the weakness of the presider's voice demand that amplification be used, the altar is never the place for a microphone. A wireless microphone (worn by the presider) is the only solution.

The Communion Rite at Sunday Mass provides ample guidance about bread and wine for the Mass: how the bread can be made by parishioners, the importance of having enough bread and enough wine at every celebration, and many related questions. That book can be used also as a catechetical tool.

The topic of bread and wine that meet the requirements established and the vessels to contain them is worthy of attention before any other matters relating to objects and decoration for worship. Bread and wine, fruit of the earth, work of human hands, gifts of God, are foundational for us as Catholics. The desire for convenience has led us to minimize the bread and do without the cup for the assembly, but convenience should have no place at this table.

The kind and quality of the bread matter. The kind and quality and quantity of the wine matter. We are a people who believe in the sacramentality of creation. We are not about magic but about sacrament. Thus we deny something at the heart of being Catholic when we give in to convenience, when we are satisfied with thin, mass-produced wafers, or when we have wine only for the presider. When we give in to convenience, we perpetrate a magical approach to the liturgy that is also a minimalist approach: God will be satisfied if we have just this tiny wafer, these few drops of wine. Yet eating and drinking are essential to what we do here.

We know from the sadder parts of our history what happens when the assembly is denied eating and drinking of the eucharistic body and blood of Christ. In centuries past, the assembly, refused access to the table, sought something at least to see. But the scripture and the tradition on which we are founded are not about visual adoration but about our Lord telling us to "take this, all of you, and eat it" and "take this, all of you, and drink it." (For marvelous examples of homiletic reflection on these elements of our rite, see Photina Rech's *Wine and Bread*.)

If the eucharistic prayer is to become the vital force for making Catholics, then the table and the bread and wine matter greatly. The bread and wine are to be handled with great reverence in the preparation of the table, and during the eucharistic prayer are to be seen as food and drink for this assembly.

Posture of the Assembly

At present the universal church has no single approach to this, nor perhaps should it. The *General Instruction of the Roman Missal* calls for standing during the eucharistic prayer except during the institution narrative. The American bishops' appendix to this document calls for kneeling after the Holy, Holy to the end of the prayer in the dioceses of the United States. The *General Instruction* itself recognizes that there may be reasons for the assembly to remain standing throughout the prayer. It is a question that will be resolved with increased experience.

The basic resource for historical background is *The Posture of the Assembly during the Eucharistic Prayer* by Nathan Mitchell and John Leonard. This book traces the early church's practice of standing, especially on the Lord's Day, a practice that gradually ended as the liturgy came to be seen as the work of the clergy while the laity stayed at a distance and prayed silently. This is the centuries-long shift from the active engagement of all in praise and thanksgiving around the table to the assembly's distant adoration of the consecrated bread and wine. Vatican II drew from the ancient tradition in calling for full, conscious and active participation in the eucharistic prayer. It remains for the current generation to translate that into steady practices in such things as posture at this prayer.

Even if standing is the posture only during the preface, give attention in this year to how the assembly stands. Too often we lean, we slouch, we fold our arms, we shift from one foot to another. That is not how people stand when they are intent on a deed. Any acolytes and other ministers who are visible to the assembly should be models of this, as should the choir (turned now toward the altar, not toward the piano or leader).

The faithful are called in the Roman canon the *omnium circumstantes,* "all those who stand around" this table. That may be a poetic description, but it should reflect reality. In the typical parish today, the assembly is not *stantes,* "standing," and the assembly is not *circum,* "around." Yet even when the assembly is placed theater-like in pews, all facing the same direction, something is still possible. This would flow from all the catechesis that takes place, in homilies and other settings, about the eucharistic prayer during this year. Those who wish might be invited forward to stand around the table, leaving the side toward the pews open, of course, so that no one's vision is blocked.

Some parishes have invited children to come forward in this way, but this is never a good idea. It must be an open invitation, extended after the prayer over the gifts and before "The Lord be with you." (The movement of people then serves also to give the eucharistic prayer a distinct beginning which it often now does not have. This is so because the presider would wait until all who wish have come forward.) A variation on this would be possible in those assemblies where the money and other gifts for the poor are brought forward by the people in formal or informal procession. Those who wish, or perhaps all, could simply remain in the area around the altar as the rest of the preparation is made for the eucharistic prayer.

The danger is that this divides the assembly in two. But at least the appearance of division can be avoided if the people arrange themselves at the table in such a way that they extend from the two far edges of the pews toward and around the altar. Then there is a surrounding, not a division into "us" and "them."

This suggestion of coming forward is rooted not only in the ancient practice but in the assembly's pastoral need: We need to see each other's faces. When we surround the table, we become conscious of ourselves as the body of Christ in a way we cannot be when our visual perception is limited to the backs of heads. What happens then is risky. Distraction is possible, though only a little more likely than in any other arrangement of the assembly. But a certain serious wonder is also possible: Here is my assembled church in all its diversity of age and size and sex and background and wealth and politics. We look toward our altar, toward our bread and wine, and beyond it we see the church, and we know that we are being seen as church by others. This can inspire rather than distract.

In no way does this arrangement of the assembly detract from the unique status of the ordained minister (who is vested and who clearly leads this prayer). And it certainly is not true that this arrangement of the assembly means that we are no longer worshiping God but each other. Those who claim this miss the point.

Finding the best posture is one of those efforts to build our participation that cannot be judged until it has been in place for months, and this after much catechesis.

Catechesis for the Assembly

The core group during this year needs to look toward homilies that will draw on the eucharistic prayer. In the first place, that should mean that homilists, whatever the central thrust of the homily, draw on some words or images from one of the eucharistic prayers. But it also means that sometimes the homily itself can be about the centrality and the wealth of this prayer. So, on some Sundays of this year there should be an opportunity to make the eucharistic prayer itself the "text" of the homily. This "text" is not only the eucharistic prayer's words and acclamation but its gestures, its bread and wine.

Catechize the assembly

There is much to explore, as all of the above notes illustrate. Models can be found in *Preaching about the Mass* and *Saving Signs, Wondrous Words.* This may in many parishes be a "why didn't anyone ever tell us about this before?" situation, at least if it is done with the understanding, love and zeal for the liturgy that good liturgical preaching presumes. Each of the moments of the eucharistic prayer could be unfolded by looking at texts from the current prayers, by speaking on one Sunday of thanksgiving, on another of what it means to ask God to send the Holy Spirit upon the gifts and to transform us, on another of the work of remembering, on another of sacrifice and offering, on another of why we include intercession in these prayers and what that intercession is to be. The words of the opening dialogue and all the words of acclamations, including the Amen, would find their way into several of these homilies. So would a pondering of bread and wine, of eating and drinking.

The hope in such homilies or in catechesis at any level is never to explain the ritual, as one would explain some practice like shaking hands or some established convention like driving on the right side of the road, for our rites are not puzzles to be solved and understood. The rites, including the rite we call the eucharistic prayer, are too large and too deep and even too broad for explanation. Instead, the homilist asks us to ponder some moment of the ritual, usually some play of words, tune, gesture, objects and the way they intersect and interact among us. "Here is what we say and do at such and such a time in our liturgy. What is your experience of this moment? What from our scriptures and what from our other rituals and our arts and our teachings are echoed here?"

Sometimes the history of a word or of a particular practice can be helpful. Sometimes it is useful to ponder the way some religious rituals do in fact have their parallels in other parts of life (for example, we have entrance rites of sorts in everyday life, in political and legal forums, in sports). Throughout, the homilist is not teaching facts to students but inviting the assembly to engage in a conversation with God by taking to themselves their own rites. The homilist seeks ways to ponder with the assembly: "Here, sisters and brothers, is what we do (we say Amen, we process, we keep silence); can we together imagine what sort of deed this is and what sort of people we who do it are becoming?"

During the time that the parish ponders and works at its practice of the eucharistic prayer, homilists can also pay attention to the ways Catholics have prayed and can pray from the eucharist in daily lives. They can explore the ways that we bless God and bless ourselves and bless our food: the signs we make, the words we say. Even the simplest forms of morning and evening prayer are generally first of all prayers of praise and thanksgiving, echoes of the eucharistic prayer of the Lord's Day. Those who have never learned this part of the tradition can be invited to learn it now and to begin little by little to learn prayers and psalms of praise and thanksgiving. House-holds, whatever their shape and whether they have one or a dozen members, can be offered some forms of meal prayer and meal practice that enrich the traditional "Bless us, O Lord."

The core group may wish to examine the scriptures of this entire year and select those Sundays that will lend themselves best to this preaching about the eucharistic prayer. Or they may simply set aside a number of Sundays dictated more by the need to do this work than by appropriateness of the scriptures. There is no need to apologize for this, as the homily can always be based on parts of the liturgy.

The Sundays of Easter season would be in any year a most appropriate time to ponder the eucharistic praying of the church. Another excellent time, if this happens to be Year B, would be those summer Sundays when the gospel readings are taken from John 6, the bread of life discourse.

As in all these years, the homily and bulletin are by no means the only catechesis. Those who teach children and engage youth and adults in education should take their cue from what is decided about the preaching on Sunday and then explore ways in which their own work can incorporate some of the contents and directions of this work. The third grade in the parish school, the first communion preparation group, the Monday-night youth group, adults who meet to reflect on scripture: All should be invited in the course of this year to ponder the eucharistic prayer and learn more of their Catholic tradition and responsibility.

Implement the changes

Implement the changes

List the particular changes you will undertake.	Beginning date	Check-up date

∾ **Resources** to Gather for Year Four

All of these resources are available from Liturgy Training Publications: 1-800-933-1800. Those marked with an asterisk (*) can be found in the anthology *The Liturgy Documents, Volume One.*

Roman Documents

*Constitution on the Sacred Liturgy**

*General Instruction of the Roman Missal**

Lectionary for Mass: Introduction *

U.S. Documents

*Fulfilled in Your Hearing**

*Music in Catholic Worship**

Pastoral Letter of Cardinal Roger Mahony *Gather Faithfully Together* (also available as *Guide for Sunday Mass,* in English and Spanish)

Pastoral Letter of Cardinal Joseph Bernardin *Our Communion, Our Peace, Our Promise* (also available as *Guide for the Assembly,* in English and Spanish)

Books

Martin Connell, *Guide to the Revised Lectionary*

Edward Foley, *Preaching Basics*

Diana Kodner, *Handbook for Cantors*

Gabe Huck, *Preaching about the Mass*

David Philippart, *Saving Signs, Wondrous Words*

Aelred Rosser, *A Well-Trained Tongue: Formation in the Ministry of Reader*

Aelred Rosser, *Guide for Lectors*

Short Commentaries on the Documents

"Overview of the *Lectionary for Mass:* Introduction" by Gerard Sloyan*

Videos

Proclaiming the Word: Formation for Readers in the Liturgy

Video Guide to Gather Faithfully Together

The Word of the Lord (part three of *The Sunday Mass Series)*

Year Four
The Liturgy of the Word

Wherever Christians go, we carry our scriptures. And when Christians gather, we open the scriptures and read or chant aloud and then ponder what we have heard. And from this, there comes all dimensions of Christian prayer. The scriptures, read by and within the assembled church, bind us together, bind us across the centuries past and future. Engaging the scriptures together, we find our identity and our mission.

The lectionary is a way of ordering the scriptures for reading at liturgy. In these first generations following Vatican II, there is perhaps no greater testimony to the need for the Council's liturgical reforms than the way the lectionary has been received in parishes. In many parishes the liturgy of the word is done well, and this has meant nothing short of a revolution in Catholic life: a recovery of the centrality of scripture.

Because so much has been done well in the reform of the liturgy of the word, this work is suggested for Year Four. By now, the hardest and most satisfying work on the parish Sunday liturgy has been done, and with some modest additional effort, parish practices for the liturgy of the word can now be improved.

The liturgy of the word begins when the assembly has said Amen to the opening prayer, and it ends when the assembly

has said Amen to the prayer that concludes the general intercessions. This is that portion of the Sunday liturgy understood
now to be foundation of all else. On this foundation stands the
liturgy of the eucharist. When the liturgy of the word is strong,
the liturgy of eucharist can be done with a similar strength. But
when there is no foundation, no worthy liturgy of the word,
little can be done. The challenges may be these:

- *The liturgy of the word begins before anyone is ready to listen (that's really an entrance rite problem).*

- *Readers, including gospel readers, do not prepare or do not
have the gifts for public proclamation.*

- *There is no dependable, sturdy flow to the rite Sunday after
Sunday, no rhythm of sound and silence, of spoken and sung,
of stillness and procession.*

- *Homilists do not prepare sufficiently or do not have the gift
for preaching.*

- *Little attention is given to the general intercessions, which
are read from a "canned" source and could be prayers said
in any community on any day rather than the prayers of this
parish at this particular hour, with all that is happening in
the world and the neighborhood.*

Behind these may be other areas to confront:

- *Our sense for scripture, including the psalms, is still
elementary.*

- *We find it hard to understand listening as an active role; the
assembly easily becomes passive, an audience, during the
liturgy of the word.*

Here is the general approach to each of these years
applied to this year of work on the liturgy of the word:

- *Using some of the resources listed below (and on page 93),
and using this chapter itself as a starting point, the core*

group explores the rite: the history, the ministries involved, the present practice, other practices. The first step in that exploration for most groups will be growing in knowledge of the lectionary. After this, the group can take a look at the rite as a whole, then spend other sessions focused on various elements that need work: for example, the way in which the gospel procession and acclamation are and could be done, the training of lectors, the preparation of homilies. As in other years, the important element in these discussions will be mystagogy: discovering how people can speak from their own experience about the mystery we celebrate. Along the way, only this chapter itself need be read by all. Other reading can be divided: different people read from different resources and then report to the whole group. Discussions should be held at least once a month.

- *These discussions will unfold the strengths and the shortcomings of the present practice. Notes of key observations should be made along the way, along with points of consensus. Experiences should be shared and pondered. Throughout these discussions, those responsible should inject the key insights of the appropriate documents: What does the church intend to do when it celebrates the liturgy of the word? Through this process, the group will come to the questions: Can we envision the best celebration of the liturgy of the word and the steps we must take to get there?*

- *Resources and occasions for broader catechesis should be explored. This is to be directed at those who minister in the liturgy of the word: lectors, cantors and other musicians, presiders, deacons, acolytes, homilists. But catechesis is also necessary for the whole assembly. These discussions should always consider how coming seasons and the readings themselves may offer good occasions for catechesis. The core group will want to ponder these questions: What is the spectrum of familiarity with the Bible in our parish? What efforts have been or are being made to know the Bible better? How aware are parishioners of the structure of the lectionary? What efforts have been made to help people prepare for Sunday liturgy by reading the Sunday scriptures in preparation or as follow-through? Likewise, do the psalms, our most basic prayers and songs, have any life in the parish apart from their brief appearance on Sundays?*

- *The nature of the liturgy of the word—that is, the central place of scripture in the life of the assembly and of each individual—means that in this year more will probably be done about what happens apart from the liturgy. But the renewal of the parish's liturgy of the word is essential so that Sunday by Sunday the assembly, through participation in this liturgy, is caught up in love for God's word.*

- *After preparation and catechesis, how will implementation take place, all at once or one element at a time? What continuing catechesis will be offered?*

- *Finally, great attention is needed as implementation begins. For example, as silence is introduced after each of the first two readings at every Sunday liturgy, the parish cantors (usually the ones who determine when to move from silence to psalm or acclamation) will have to determine how they can make the length of the silence consistent from Mass to Mass and from week to week. In every adjustment to the parish's liturgy of the word, patience and firmness will be necessary, as will evaluation and thoughtful critique.*

    The core group should attend to this: In any effort to draw parishioners into reading and study of the Bible, those who work in religious education (in schools, non-school programs and with teens and adults in Bible studies, small-group reflection, sacramental preparation or other activities) are already doing an important part of this work. Here, more than other areas of the liturgy, we can see how liturgy and catechesis flow back and forth. Both are constantly involved with the Bible. Scripture is foundational when we are teaching and when we are gathered on Sunday.

Resources

 Behind the parish effort to do justice to the liturgy of the word is a Roman document that served to introduce the 1981 edition of the lectionary. This is usually referred to simply as the Introduction to the *Lectionary for Mass.* More than any book about the liturgy of the word, this document can guide the work of the core group. It can be found in lectionaries that were revised beginning (in the United States) at the end of 1998. It can also be found in *The Liturgy Documents, Volume One* (LTP) with a brief but important overview written by Gerard Sloyan.

If, as suggested above, the core group begins with an examination of the lectionary itself, *Guide to the Revised Lectionary* (LTP) by Martin Connell can serve as a supplemental text. The most important step is understanding why we have a lectionary at all, and how the present lectionary is structured, with its strengths and weaknesses. In studying this book, the core group will explore the role of the lectionary in giving expression to the different seasons of the liturgical year and to Ordinary Time. Various charts provide an overview of how each gospel and letter of the New Testament is read in the three-year cycle. In the course of this lectionary study, the group will become aware that we Catholics share a basic pattern of scripture reading with Episcopalians, Lutherans, Presbyterians, Methodists and some other Protestant churches. On most Sundays, we are reading the same scriptures. In some communities, that can foster ecumenical dialogue.

In its study of the movement through the liturgy of the word itself, the Introduction to the *Lectionary for Mass* (especially chapter two) can be studied with the notes that follow in this chapter. In addition, the following will be helpful:

The short passages from the following two books could be read together:

From *Preaching about the Mass,* "The Liturgy of the Word I," pages 22–31; "The Liturgy of the Word II," pages 33–41	**Assigned to:**
Saving Signs, Wondrous Words, "Alleluia!" pages 1–3; "The Word of the Lord. Thanks Be to God!" pages 15–17; "Keeping Silence," pages 21–23; "Let Us Pray to the Lord," pages 24–27	_____
	_____

All would benefit from viewing together *The Word of the Lord* (part three of *The Sunday Mass Series*).

When it comes time to reflect on the various ministries of the liturgy of the word, there are many resources. Among those that will be helpful are:

Handbook for Cantors	**Assigned to:**
A Well-Trained Tongue: Formation in the Ministry of Reader	
Guide for Lectors	_____
Preaching Basics	
Proclaiming the Word: Formation for Readers in the Liturgy (video)	_____
	_____

In the beginning and throughout, these portions of documents are important:

Assigned to:	
_____	*Constitution on the Sacred Liturgy,* 24, 28–29, 35, 51–52, 56
	General Instruction of the Roman Missal, 33–47, 89–99, 131–32, 148–52
_____	*Lectionary for Mass:* Introduction, with overview by Gerard Sloyan, pages 118–23 in *The Liturgy Documents, Volume One*
	Fulfilled in Your Hearing
_____	*Music in Catholic Worship,* 45, 55, 63

The Liturgy of the Word: An Overview

Plan changes

The first true business of the assembled church on the Lord's Day is to hear the word of God. This is so whatever the circumstances of a particular church: whether things are better or worse, richer or poorer, in sickness or in health. We do not search the scriptures to find the "right" text for the mood or happenings of the particular day. Instead, we read from the appointed place. The church stands under the scriptures.

The work of this year is to bring the assembly to do their liturgy of the word fully, consciously and actively. The order is this: The assembly listens to a reading that is usually from the Hebrew scriptures and, after a time of silence, joins in the back-and-forth of singing a psalm whose refrain all have come to know by heart. Then another lector reads from a New Testament letter (during Ordinary Time beginning near where we left off last week), and again silence follows. This ends with the intonation of the Alleluia, when all rise to sing while the presider or deacon (perhaps carrying high the book of the gospels) processes to the ambo accompanied by candle-carrying acolytes.

The gospel is announced, acclaimed again with the signing of forehead and lips and heart, proclaimed and again acclaimed by all as the book is kissed by the reader. Then the homilist draws the assembly into further engagement with scripture, liturgy, life and world, and again there is silence after this homily. Then, when the catechumens have been dismissed and the creed has been recited, the presider invites all to pray, and the great intercessory prayer begins, spoken or chanted back and forth as the needs of the world and the church are brought to God. At the end the presider asks that our prayers be heard through Christ our Lord. The assembly gives its Amen and the liturgy of the world has ended.

What those preparing the liturgy have to understand is this: The liturgy of the word is not a matter of just getting various little pieces in the right order. The whole liturgy of the word has an integrity, a movement, a flow that the assembly is meant to carry Sunday after Sunday. That requires great attention to finding the pace and keeping it, to training ministers in timing and movement, as well as in the skills of public reading. It requires that we understand that this is not a time to impress, inspire or entertain the assembly; it, like all the liturgy, is the work of an assembly that knows its task by heart. Those who minister as presider, lector or cantor must, as members of the assembly themselves, know and honor the integrity of this rite, its pace, its immense importance to the church. Now we may look in greater detail.

The Readings

When the entrance rites, which probably vary greatly from one season to another, are done, all in the assembly—including the presider and every other minister—attend to the reader and the proclaimed word. Normally the transition to the liturgy of the word is marked by a change of posture: All are seated.

There is no rush. Even when the entrance rites are done well, the assembly usually needs time to settle in before the ears are ready to listen. The lector, whose place in the assembly is normally not set apart from everyone else, need not come forward until all are seated. Standing at an appointed place, an ambo (reading desk, pulpit, lectern and bema are other names for this place), the reader opens the book and begins.

This word is a spoken word to be heard by the assembly. It is never to be a time when individuals read God's word for themselves from participation aids. All eyes—including those of the presider and other ministers—are on the reader for the attention and increased understanding that visual contact brings to what is heard. If the reader is alive with what is to be spoken, then nothing is more natural for the assembly than to look directly at this person throughout the whole reading.

The reader announces the day's scripture exactly as it is announced in the lectionary; there is no need to add or take away. For members of the assembly, the challenge is to listen as the church. That is something few know how to do but all can work on together. The word is addressed to the whole church, and it is addressed to this church, this assembly. There is a corporate presence here. Individually, each person gives attention, but each is to hear with the ears and mind and heart of a member of the body of Christ. That is one of those skills we have to work on together to master. In a society that is oriented toward the individual and not the collective, it is difficult to achieve. We are moving in the right direction when only those with hearing impairments have written copies of the reading, and when the excellence of the reader draws all eyes and all attention.

There is no one right way to read the scriptures in the midst of the church. Those who are entrusted with this task usually do well when they habitually let God's word amaze and intrigue and upset them. They wrestle with that word, that passage, always alert to some single word, some phrase, some image that can bring us to life. Readers want others to hear, to be caught up in the beauty or the power or the harshness of a passage. To make this happen, they live for days and nights with the passage, knowing that much is entrusted to them.

In their public reading, the church's readers do just that: They *read!* They do not dramatize. They do not drone. They lift the words printed on paper into sounds of parables, letters, stories, warnings, poems, genealogies. Most of the time the text merely awaits someone who truly wants others to hear what they have heard.

When the lector has finished, the church reflects in silence. Both the listening and the silence are accomplished by all together. This silence needs time, at least a full minute, to take hold and to give due reverence and attention to what has been read. The reader may simply step back and stand silently during this time; this usually helps the silence more than when the reader returns at once to his or her place to be seated.

The Psalm

Out of the silence the cantor approaches the ambo and intones the psalm. Note that some churches have a minister whose only task is singing the psalm, and so this person is called the psalmist. This serves to set the singing of the psalm apart. This practice may be good in that it highlights the psalm as an integral part of the liturgy of the word and not simply another task of the cantor. But in most parishes, the cantor takes this role of psalmist as well as the other tasks needed to lead the assembly in song.

Though there are various ways in which the psalm may be sung, most assemblies are now familiar and comfortable with a "responsorial" style, in which a refrain is sung by the assembly and the psalmist or cantor sings the verses of the psalm. Singing the refrain seems to engage the assembly. An assembly seldom can speak a refrain with any power. If song is not possible, the cantor or psalmist may sing the psalm while the assembly listens. Or, if even this is not possible, the psalmist (not the lector) may read the psalm without a refrain, although the special character of the psalm is lost in this case. This is one more instance where it is clear that the liturgy of an assembly is mostly carried out in song. Only song allows the ritual to take place.

The lectionary recognizes the importance of singing or chanting the psalm when it offers seasonal psalms and refrains that can replace the "once a year" texts assigned to a given Sunday. When this is done, something is certainly lost in the way a specific psalm was intended to be juxtaposed with a given first reading, but there is also something gained: An assembly begins to know a few psalms by heart, begins to know this way of praying, and begins to associate texts and melodies with the keeping of each season. Those who help prepare the liturgy, including musicians, should carefully choose psalms to develop a sturdy repertoire that will serve one Advent after another, one July and August after another.

The psalms are our school of praying. They will not school us, though, unless the psalmist or cantor can articulate their words well. And they will not school us unless the parish helps us with psalms for praying at home. The Introduction to the lectionary says we must "turn these psalms into the prayer of the church" (#19) and presumes that the psalms will be preached and will be part of whatever catechetical practice happens in the parish. They will live on Sundays when they live day by day in people's lives. So far we have barely begun.

There is great leeway in choosing the translation to be used so that many possible melodies offer themselves. This is good as long as in any given assembly there is a priority on fine music that bears repetition. Catechists and others in the parish ought to make frequent use of these psalms when any group gathers for religious education and other study. Likewise, these are our by-heart prayers for parish meetings and other gatherings.

The psalm ends and the psalmist or cantor leaves the ambo as the reader of the second reading rises and comes forward. Only in some unforeseen circumstances should the same person proclaim both readings. This is because the readings speak in different voices at a Sunday Mass, and this difference will be heard when different lectors proclaim them. Also, it is more than enough for one person to prepare one reading for a Sunday, let alone two!

The Gospel Procession and Proclamation

The silence after the second reading should be consistent from week to week, like the silence, after the first reading. Out of this silence, a cantor or instrumentalist begins the Alleluia, at which time all—presider and acolytes included—stand. This standing can be the subject of catechesis: We are rising to acclaim the gospel of the Lord, and it is an attentive standing, a "standing at attention" of sorts. The Alleluias begin, and they are sung or are not done at all (it is impossible to "say" an Alleluia).

The singing of the Alleluia accompanies the movement of presider or deacon to the ambo for the proclamation of the gospel. When a book of the gospels has been carried into the assembly in the entrance rite and placed on the altar, the book is now lifted from the altar by the one who is to read, held high and carried to the ambo. Acolytes with candles and, at least on great feasts, with incense accompany the book. This procession need not be the shortest distance between two points. The ritual is one of acclamation and anticipation. The tradition, preserved best in the Eastern churches, is to celebrate the book that contains the gospel by carrying it through the acclaiming assembly.

When the parish has no tradition of a separate book of the gospels, one of two things can happen. Presider and acolytes could walk to the ambo while the Alleluia is sung, but it would be difficult to call this a procession, and it is hard to know what the Alleluias acclaim. Or the reader of the second reading, who has remained a step or two back from the ambo during the period of silence, can carry the lectionary to the presider. The presider then takes the lectionary, lifts it high, and with the acolytes processes to the ambo. The case can be made that even where a single book is used (and this itself is a sign of the unity of our scripture), that book can be held high and acclaimed before the gospel is read from it. The rubrics do not provide for this, but there seems to be nothing against it. In any case, an assembly needs at least one durable Alleluia chant for its gospel acclamation, and several of these would allow some seasonal variety and identity (and, of course, a chant of "Praise to you, Lord Jesus Christ" is needed for Lent).

The acclamation and the procession are a single movement. Acolytes and presider should also be singing the Alleluia, and the procession should end as the singing of the Alleluia ends, so that the presider or deacon can immediately exclaim, "The Lord be with you!" and so continue the anticipation of the gospel. The signing of the book and of the forehead, lips and heart before the gospel, and the kissing of the book after the gospel, should be done with reverence. They are part of a language of gesture that we speak too little now. When candles are held during the reading, acolytes should face the presider and attend to the reading, joining in all responses and acclamations. When incense is used at this time, the fragrant smoke should clearly be seen (and smelled) as another sign of honor to the book of the gospels. The book is left on the ambo.

The Homily

The homily's place in the liturgy of the word is ancient and vital. The word once proclaimed was to be pondered, and in various ways this is what has happened. The mission of the homily is clearly expressed in the *General Instruction of the Roman Missal:* "[The homily] should develop some point of the readings or of another text from the Ordinary or from the Proper of the Mass of the day, and take into account the mystery being celebrated and the needs proper to the listeners" (#41). Thus the homilist looks to the entire liturgy and not only the scriptures. This would certainly include prayers and psalms and songs, blessings and postures and gestures, the altar and bread and wine, and all other objects used in liturgy.

This is the approach suggested by this book when it discusses the need for catechesis for and from the liturgy, and for a mystagogical conversation and preaching that is rooted in how the liturgy itself transforms us.

In the Introduction to the lectionary, the homily is spoken of in a way that gives further support to this:

> *[The one presiding] opens their souls to gratitude for the wonderful works of God. He strengthens their faith in the word that in the celebration becomes a sacrament through the Holy Spirit. Finally, he prepares them for a fruitful reception of communion and invites them to embrace the demands of the Christian life. (#41)*

The qualities of homilist and homily are much discussed in other places. What is important here (as the core group focuses for a year on the liturgy of the word and on parish practice) is to establish sustainable ways to improve the current state of preaching. Preaching is a liturgical act, not a time-out, and it is too important to be left out of the parish's effort at liturgical renewal.

In many places this would mean studying the U.S. bishops' document *Fulfilled in Your Hearing* and especially its recommendation (#106–8) that homilists become part of "homily preparation groups" that meet weekly or seasonally. These are small groups of parishioners who gather to read and reread the scriptures of a Sunday or a season to ponder them. The goal is not to write or even outline the homily but to invigorate the homilist. This proposal is further developed by Edward Foley in *Preaching Basics* (available from LTP).

Like the first two readings, the homily is followed by a time of silent reflection.

Dismissals, the Creed and the Intercessions

Before the gathered church can go on to the creed and intercessions, to the eucharistic prayer and to sharing in holy communion, those who are catechumens or elect are dismissed. In some parishes, this means a dismissal every Sunday, even in Eastertime, because some inquirers and catechumens are always present. The more this simple but important rite of dismissal is consistent at Sunday Mass, the more the assembly will become aware of the work of evangelization, of the centrality of baptism, of their own rights and duties at Sunday Mass.

This dismissal, the model for which is found in the *Rite of Christian Initiation of Adults,* begins to restore a discipline of the eucharist. It is not simply about who can approach holy communion (or else it could happen at the Lord's Prayer or after the peace greeting) but about the right and duty of the baptized to intercede, to pray the eucharistic prayer, exchange the peace greeting and finally to share in holy communion. The right and duty to engage in all these deeds, received in baptism, becomes more and more a part of the assembly's self-understanding when we dismiss with prayer those who are not yet baptized.

The dismissal itself needs no elaboration (see RCIA, 136, for examples). The catechumens are sent forth to continue pondering the scriptures with their catechists. They and the entire assembly are reminded that we await that day when they join the baptized at the Lord's table.

Following the dismissal, the assembly vigorously recites the creed. Immediately after the creed, the presider invites all to join in the intercessions. The presider's words here are not to be a prayer but an exhortation. Then the presider and all others in the assembly give attention to the cantor or another minister who chants or reads the prayers of intercession.

The restoration of the intercessions or prayer of the faithful was called for in the *Constitution on the Sacred Liturgy* itself:

Especially on Sundays and holy days of obligation there is to be restored, after the gospel and the homily, "the universal prayer" or "the prayer of the faithful." By this prayer, in which the people are to take part, intercession shall be made for holy church, for the civil authorities, for those oppressed by various needs, for all people, and for the salvation of the entire world. (#53)

The *General Instruction of the Roman Missal* gives this further directive:

The people, exercising their priestly function, intercede for all humanity. . . . It belongs to the priest celebrant to direct the general intercessions, by means of a brief introduction to invite the congregation to pray, and after the intercessions to say the concluding prayer. It is desirable that a deacon, cantor, or other person announce the intentions. The whole assembly gives expression to its supplication either by a response said together after each intention or by a silent prayer. (#45, 47)

Though various Christian traditions, including especially the Orthodox churches, have rituals that foster the participatory prayer these directives envision, Roman Catholic churches have mostly settled for something far less. Dull would understate these moments in the liturgy at most parishes. What the church once clearly understood as a right and a duty of the baptized now slips by almost unnoticed.

The task of renewal is to establish a mode of praying that allows these prayers to bring the liturgy of the word to a strong conclusion. Having listened to God's word and having reflected on that word and having dismissed those who are not baptized, the church now takes on what is basic to our presence in the world: to stand before God and lift up all the needs of the world. If that is done with attention, with the rituals that engage all, then members of the assembly begin to realize that this is what we Christians do. We keep our eyes on all that cries out for God's attention, and we bring these things to God.

The presider's role, as noted above, is first of all to call the assembly to prayer. This is not itself a prayer. It is addressed to the assembly, not to God. It need not be a summary of the homily, it need not be new each Sunday. It is a strong and urgent call to prayer, like "Let us pray" earlier in the liturgy. Sometimes those three words may be all that is needed here.

The intercessions themselves usually consist (as on Good Friday) of a cantor or another announcing one by one some of those things that are urgent for us. After that announcement comes the ritual address to the assembly, often "Let us pray to the Lord." The assembly's task is to do just that: to pray. "Lord, have mercy" or "Lord, hear our prayer" are traditional forms. Only the assembly addresses God. The cantor or reader addresses the assembly.

Two things are important and greatly neglected: the ritual form these intercessions take, and the quality of the text. This kind of praying is like a litany, a call-and-response in which the call keeps changing (except for the constant conclusion) and the response stays the same. As anyone who has experienced a litany (the litany of the saints or of the Blessed Virgin Mary, for example) prayed in a spoken voice and the same litany chanted, we know which one engages us in prayer. The chant gives a rhythm and an ability to enter into the prayer as an assembly. It is hardly possible to imagine the many intercessory litanies of the Orthodox liturgy being read in a spoken voice. It would be like speaking "Happy birthday to you." Yet parishes continue to treat the intercessions as spoken prayers and assemblies continue to find them utterly forgettable.

In its effort to achieve participation (and the formation of an interceding people) in the Sunday intercessions, parishes can look to several models for the call-and-response. These can be tried for a season (Lent, Easter) until the parish has two or three forms, one for Ordinary Time and one or more for the different seasons. Both call and response are places in which multilingual parishes can use different languages without repetition of one in the others.

Many sources offer suggested texts for the intercessions. These sources vary greatly in quality. It works well when one person in the parish, a person who knows a good sentence from a poor one, is in charge of preparing these texts. That person can draw on any source that is well written and that shows some understanding of the needs for which the church should intercede. But local additions will always be necessary. There is no need whatsoever to come up with new texts every week. A good call for prayer will be a good call for prayer week after week. But the season, the lectionary, the life of the parish (including by name, when possible, the sick and those who have recently died) and the life of the world in the past week and the week to come, all come to bear on what will be the text of a given Sunday. Once prepared, this text should be accessible to the one who chants or reads it so that it can be prepared with care.

If the parish has the practice of placing a book in the entrance area where people can write their intentions for prayer, then the prepared text can be placed in this book, and the book can be carried forward by the cantor or reader. Among the intercessions can be one for "all that is written in this book of intercession and all we name in our hearts."

The presider concludes this with a prayer (but never begins by saying "Let us pray"—that is what the assembly has been doing). This prayer need never be a repetition of what has been said. It is an Amen to all that has gone before. This can be a prayer composed and prepared for each Sunday, or it can be one of several good texts that bear repetition Sunday after Sunday. The examples in the sacramentary itself are useful.

Some sort of pause is necessary. If the ushers are already in place for taking up the collection, the gift bearers already approaching the presider or the acolytes already carrying the cup and corporal to the altar, we lose the sense that with the intercessions we have concluded our liturgy of the word. It may be as simple as all sitting down together for the briefest silence before the preparation of the gifts begins.

Before ending the discussion of the liturgy of the word, what about people who arrive after the liturgy begins? Some parishes don't allow people to take their places once the reader has announced the first reading. Instead, people gather in the entrance area until the assembly stands for the gospel acclamation, then ushers help late-comers take places within the assembly.

The only good alternative to this is to keep some rows of benches or chairs near the entrance free, roped off until the liturgy of the word begins. Then late-comers can fill these without too much disturbance. This practice comes easier when parish practice already encourages people who arrive first to take the places closest to the table.

Hospitality and common sense can clash in a parish's struggle with this question. Hospitality says: Don't be judgmental, and don't penalize folks who are late. Common sense says: If this assembly is to have a chance of listening well, then don't have people moving up and down the aisles and into places while the reader is reading. Both are important. Maybe people in the assembly can work this one out for themselves during the year.

The Ministries

Train the ministers Those who minister in the liturgy of the word—lectors and gospel readers, cantors, homilists—need ongoing attention to their ministries. If this has been neglected, then this year must see it begin. Resources for these ministries are numerous; some were named above. It goes beyond the scope of this book to be specific about the training of these ministers, but clearly the liturgy of the word is hampered if readers cannot read well, cantors cannot handle the singing of psalms, and homilists irritate people for all the wrong reasons (which is not to be confused with making people, the homilist included, uncomfortable with the gospel's demands).

One specific thing all these ministers must know is that they are members of the assembly and as such must themselves be attentive listeners to the scriptures, singers of the psalm refrains, makers of intercession. Nothing cuts at the assembly's participation so much as seeing a minister who is clearly not being attentive during the reading.

The importance of having the scriptures proclaimed well has led some parishes to offer weekly times when the readers (including gospel readers) for the next Sunday can practice and even discuss the scriptures. The importance of having good preaching has likewise led to weekly, monthly or seasonal sessions during which all those who preach read and ponder the scriptures for a given Sunday or season together. These are times to savor the scriptures, to ask one another: "Why this particular word?" "What does that turn of phrase mean?" "Why did this happen and not that?" The best sessions are those that really grapple with the texts rather than quickly rush off to some easy application.

In working with the various ministers of the liturgy of the word, use the resources listed on page 93. Distribute copies of the various guides to each group of ministers. Ask the coordinator of each ministry to set up a time for discussion of the material and/or the viewing of the videotapes. This can be in lieu of the annual ministry day, or, if there hasn't been an annual ministry day, the first one.

Catechesis for the Assembly

Catechize the assembly

The assembly should also receive catechesis about the liturgy of the word this year. As in other years, this can take various forms (bulletin articles, discussions in youth and adult education sessions, discussions with catechists and ministers), but the Sunday homily is crucial for the widest communication. And these homilies, as in other years, can take the form of a series at some appropriate place in the year. Lent, for example, is always an appropriate time to address how the baptized and those preparing for baptism take part in the liturgy of the word and let that word shape their lives. Such homilies, as has been said, have the nature of mystagogy—reflecting together on the mystery we celebrate. They are less about informing an audience and more about engaging an assembly in collective remembering and reflection. Models are given in *Preaching about the Mass.* Catechists in school, religious education and youth groups should be involved in planning how this will be given shape in their work.

In many cases it will be helpful, in discussion or in writing, to acquaint people with the structure of the lectionary (see especially *Guide to the Revised Lectionary* by Martin Connell). Even week by week the homilists can build an awareness of how the gospel of one evangelist is read through in a year, how the letters of the New Testament are read through. Sometimes the assembly can be encouraged to pursue all that surrounds a given reading from the Hebrew scriptures: What's going to happen next to Abraham? Read about it in the your Bible at home.

The following sections describe the areas that catechesis should cover during Year Four.

Listening Is an Action Done by All

We listen in one way when we are in animated conversation, and in another when we are at a play or movie or watching television. Being seated with a few hundred other people in a large room where one person opens a book and reads seems like the latter sort of situation. But it isn't. If anything, this is the "animated conversation" type of listening: alert, catching all that one can. If one is to take part, then great attention is needed.

Undoubtedly this comes easiest to an assembly whose regular homilists themselves know how to listen to scripture, how to hone in on its phrases and words, how to question it and dialogue with it, how to let the scripture be in dialogue with the songs and prayers of the liturgy, the stories and questions of the world. Regular exposure to that must shape good listeners. If the homilist is passionate about these texts of scripture, fascinated and excited by them, this will be contagious. But equally contagious is the boredom or superficiality of the homilist who has not struggled with scripture and with the language to articulate the struggle.

It is the assembly, the church, that listens to scripture at liturgy. There is a quality to this listening that makes it different from reading the same scriptures alone. The church is being addressed; the church listens. That is why the distractions of printed readings are to be avoided. In the whole liturgy of the word, the assembly never needs any printed material. The psalm refrain should be one known by heart, as should be the gospel acclamation. The response to the intercessions should be known by heart as well. The action of reading along means no listening at all takes place. If I am in this assembly, my task is not to muddle through a scripture text by myself, but to hear the living, proclaimed word of the reader, to give that person full attention as I would anyone with whom I am in conversation. Then and only then can there be some physical sense of the assembly actively listening.

Why listen? After all, it has all been read before. We've heard it. But the church has heard it for 2,000 years and still needs to hear it again, to be confronted by the scriptures, nourished by them, judged by them, given new ideas by them. Being grounded in scripture is not some nice image or lofty ideal, it has to be realized Sunday by Sunday.

Thus catechesis about the liturgy of the word will explore why the Bible is not an ornament in our homes but is opened and read daily if possible. Parish bulletins can provide suggestions for daily reading, perhaps following the weekday lectionary or guiding people in more extensive reading, especially of the Hebrew scriptures. An easily accessible parish library can provide some excellent scriptural resources in books, periodicals and videos.

If the Bible is never heard outside the church, how can it be truly heard when it is proclaimed in the liturgy? Never before have the scriptures been so readily and inexpensively available in so many translations. But have Catholics opened the book and learned to read it? Have Catholics been given down-to-earth suggestions about ways to find a steady time in daily life for a few minutes to read the Bible in the household? Some have. But one could easily come away from many conferences and religious bookstores with the impression that the Bible is but one more candidate for spirituality-of-the-month. During this year the parish could make good translations of the Bible available, or could provide books (like *At Home with the Word,* an annual publication from LTP) that present each Sunday's scriptures with reflections and actions, along with encouragement in getting these books regularly opened and enjoyed in homes.

Such familiarity with the Bible comes also from catechists in school and parish programs that are themselves informed by a good introduction to the Bible (as well as good translations and study aids). This year is the time for homilists and perhaps lectors to work together with the religious education program. It is a year to explore what sort of efforts will be productive in years to come.

Psalms Are Our Teachers of Prayer

Had the Catholic faithful never lost the psalter a lot of silly prayers might never have been written. But we did lose the psalter. The reforms of Vatican II made it again available, but all is in the hands of the parish's Sunday practice of the liturgy, and especially in the hands of the cantor and others who prepare the music. We have already discussed the merits of using the common psalms so that gradually the assembly builds a vocabulary of refrains known by heart and a familiarity with the verses of these psalms. Some assemblies can move from that to use of the lectionary's weekly psalm and let their vocabulary of psalm praying grow.

Homilists can use this year to learn the habit of listening to the psalm that the assembly will sing and hear in the liturgy of the word. In the homily, some image or verse of the psalm can be appropriately pondered. This is especially important when seasonal psalms are used for a series of weeks. A good refrain sung week after week begins to enter everyone's vocabulary. Can the homilist then be alert enough to know when a single sentence should be brought into the homily and celebrated? Can the homilist also be listening to the verses of the psalm, where the assembly may be a little less sure, and draw out those verses when they will help to build the preaching?

Even more, can homilists during this year look for opportunities when the entire homily might be an invitation to the psalter, or to some specific psalms? This can go much further if the bulletin provides suggestions for praying these at home and even gives the texts. The psalter can seem strange territory to many Catholics at first, but with a guide, it becomes not only familiar but even homey.

Beyond this, a goal for the year might be introducing a single morning psalm or canticle, a single night psalm or canticle. Psalms are also good prayers for meal time. Catechists can work with children on all or some of this, but parents and other adults can also be invited to pray and even to memorize some few verses for morning and some few verses for night. The goal is to become at home in this prayer book of synagogue and church. If the parish occasionally has morning or evening prayer, this also is an opportunity to foster a love of the psalms.

For all of these areas—household and parish morning and evening prayer, meal prayers, classroom prayers with the psalms—there are resources available. Among those available from LTP are table prayer cards for the seasons of the year, many of them making use of psalms; *Midday Prayer, Giving Thanks at the Table* and a variety of other small prayer books in which the psalms are amply used; and *Proclaim Praise*, a psalm-based morning and evening prayer for each day of the week (brief enough to be useful for beginning or ending meetings in the parish).

Intercession Is Our Duty and Our Right

In each of these areas—scripture, psalms, intercession—the task of the year is the same: restoring to Catholics something that is their baptismal right and duty. This begins to happen when the Sunday liturgy of the word itself is regularly done with full and conscious and active participation. It happens further when those who preach have a firm grasp of how fundamental these elements of the liturgy of the word are to the homily and to Catholic life and piety. It continues as the parish supports with example and with resources those ways in which parishioners can bring Bible, psalter and daily intercession into their homes and their lives.

Applying this to catechesis about intercession means building an understanding that the church itself, morning and night, prays to God for all the needy of the world, prays for God's blessing and protection. Perhaps the homilist can bring the assembly to a sense for their constant corporate work of being a voice calling for God's mercy. What is involved here is the way the baptized are bound up in loving the world as God loves the world, and so having this sometimes tedious habit of rehearsing all that's wrong, all that's in trouble, all that God seems to be forgetting. The psalms, again, are our teachers.

Implement the changes

List the particular changes you will undertake.	Beginning date	Check-up date

❧ **Resources** to Gather for Year Five

All of these resources are available from Liturgy Training Publications: 1-800-933-1800. Those marked with an asterisk (*) can be found in the anthology *The Liturgy Documents, Volume One.*

Roman Documents

*Constitution on the Sacred Liturgy**

*General Instruction of the Roman Missal**

*Directory for Masses with Children**

U.S. Documents

*Environment and Art in Catholic Worship**

Built of Living Stones

*Music in Catholic Worship**

Pastoral Letter of Cardinal Roger Mahony *Gather Faithfully Together* (also available as *Guide for Sunday Mass,* in English and Spanish)

Pastoral Letter of Cardinal Joseph Bernardin *Our Communion, Our Peace, Our Promise* (also available as *Guide for the Assembly,* in English and Spanish)

Books

Lawrence Mick, *Guide for Ushers and Greeters*

Gabe Huck, *Preaching about the Mass*

David Philippart, *Saving Signs, Wondrous Words*

David Philippart, *Serve God with Gladness: A Manual for Servers*

Videos

Video Guide to Gather Faithfully Together

We Shall Go Up with Joy (part two of *The Sunday Mass Series*)

Year Five

Entrance and Concluding Rites

You may have had to deal with these transitional rites along the way and so find little left to tend to in the final year of this renewal scheme. Nevertheless, with much else in place, the beginning and the ending need study and evaluation, and often some work.

"Transitional" is the key notion here. These are rituals that move us from one place to another, one mode to another. That is their task. How is the assembly to become an assembly? How are these several hundred diverse persons to become an assembly ready and eager to hear God's word? And how are those who have spent good time engaged in word and eucharist to take leave of this work and move back to so many different lives? Such questions arise only when one has become thoroughly convinced that this Sunday Mass is the task of all present. Before that, one has no way to question what "work" a rite has to do.

In this section we will deal first and most thoroughly with the entrance rite, saving the dismissal and concluding rites for a brief treatment at the end, and we will ask questions and raise concerns like:

• *Why worry about the entrance rites?*

- *When these rites do not take those gathered and make of them an assembly, what will?*

- *When a presider doesn't know how to handle his role here, there's no making up for it later.*

- *When the entrance rites do not announce the season, all other announcements will be merely informational.*

- *Even the best of readers will find it difficult to make God's word come through to the church that isn't ready to listen.*

What are some things that plague the entrance rites? One possible list includes

- *a song no one has sung before*

- *a song that has been sung before but shouldn't have been*

- *a song, especially one that's worth singing, that ends at the moment the presider reaches the place from which presiding happens (without respect for the song's own dynamic)*

- *a presider who is robotic in his movement*

- *a presider who seems to be auditioning for a spot on the nightly news*

- *a procession that moves too fast*

- *a procession that nobody sees*

- *the arrival of half of the assembly during the entrance rites*

- *an opening prayer read as if the presider either had never seen it before or finds it utterly dull*

- *a rote string of things—procession, sign of the cross, greeting, Kyrie, Gloria, invitation to prayer, prayer, Amen—with no flow to it*

More could be added. Vulnerable would be a good adjective for our entrance rites, yet their work is so important and so practically possible.

The challenge to the core group this year differs a bit from the previous years but will still include the following:

- *Using some of the resources listed below (and on page 121), and using this chapter itself as a starting point, the core group will explore the rite: the documents' notion of the purpose and shape of the entrance rite; the ministries involved and present practice; the whole experience that parishioners have—from waking up until the lector announces the reading—of entering into the assembly and its liturgy; the crucial task of ushers in the entrance. Even a single discussion should begin to reveal the strengths and weaknesses of present practice. Problems of the presider's leadership need to be aired honestly. All the ways the entrance rites vary from season to season should be examined. The questions that hover over the entire discussion are: Do these rites take us from all our individual lives and make of us an assembly? Do these rites, season by season, prepare this assembly to listen well to God's word?*

- *As in other years, the important element in these discussions will be mystagogy: discovering how people can speak from their own experience about the mystery we celebrate. Along the way, only this chapter itself need be read by all. Other readings can be divided: different people read from different resources and then report to the whole group. Discussions should be held at least once a month.*

- *The core group might then address the entrance rites for the Sundays in Ordinary Time. What are the strengths and weaknesses of present practice? What are legitimate alternatives to present practice? What ministries would be involved? Later discussions can focus on each of the seasons. Depending on practice to date, this might mean a great change from rites that have made no effort to embody the season to rites that strive to make our seasons tangible in the words, songs and movement. Gimmicks are to be avoided, although this is sometimes difficult. What is needed is a way of entering the liturgy of a season that will stand up to repetition. Plans would be made to prepare carefully all of the ministers involved. This has to involve practice, not with the acolytes one day and other ministers the next, but all together so that they learn it together and together can facilitate rather than distract from the assembly's work.*

- *The catechesis for the assembly should accompany the beginning of each new season in this year. It could be introduced through bulletin articles and announcements and perhaps even in the homily. Once into the season, the homilist should integrate the new practices into preaching about Advent, Christmas, Lent or the Easter season. This is not done as if the assembly were an audience to the entrance rite, but as reflection with the assembly on what it is that we all are doing here together to ready ourselves for eucharist in Advent or in Lent. Finally, there must be evaluation until things are as they should be, and care that there is consistency from Mass to Mass, week to week, one Advent or Lent to another Advent or Lent.*

Resources

The following sections of resources in use since Year One are helpful to this year's discussions and preparations:

Read and study

Gather Faithfully Together (Guide for Sunday Mass), 39–51, 78 *Our Communion, Our Peace, Our Promise (Guide for the Assembly)*, 22–34	**Assigned to:** _____ _____ _____

All would benefit in this final year by viewing the following videos together:

Assigned to:	*Video Guide to Gather Faithfully Together.* Watch the whole video again, but pay special attention to the first part that depicts the gathering and entrance rites.
_____	*We Shall Go Up with Joy* (part two of *The Sunday Mass Series*)
_____	
_____	

These short passages from the following books could be read together:

Assigned to:	*Preaching about the Mass,* "The Assembly," pages 2–11; "The Gathering Rite," pages 12–21
_____	*Saving Signs, Wondrous Words,* "I Will Bow and Be Simple," pages 7–10; "Go Up with Joy," pages 70–73; "I Am the Gate," pages 74–76; "Enter with Thanks and Praise," pages 77–80; "This Community Now Sends You Forth," pages 81–84; "Go, You Are Sent," pages 85–87
_____	
_____	

Also, the following sections from these documents should be read:

Assigned to:	*Constitution on the Sacred Liturgy,* 14
	General Instruction of the Roman Missal, 24–32, 57, 82–88, 123, 236, 270
_____	*Directory for Masses with Children,* 34, 40
	Environment and Art in Catholic Worship, 59–61
_____	*Built of Living Stones,* 95–99
_____	*Music in Catholic Worship,* 44, 49, 61, 66, 73

Thinking about Entrance

How do we enter? Think about all the entrances we customarily make just on a normal workday. We enter the day itself. We enter a place of work and the work itself. Perhaps we attend a meeting or two. Then we head home after work and spend time at table. Maybe we go to the grocery store or the home of friends. Finally, we enter the final moments of the day, then into bed for rest. Of course we often say simply: I wake up. I go to work. I eat lunch. I attend a meeting. I go home. I eat dinner. I go to bed. But we don't just do these things. Entrances are more than physically getting from one place to another.

This must be clear about our Sunday Mass entrance rites: The entrance rite is about the entrance of the assembly into their liturgy. It is not about the entrance of the ministers into the midst of the assembly. If an entrance is to be made, then the assembly must make it. It can't be done to them or for them. If we are not engaged by our entrance rites, then there is no entrance, the assembly never assembled, the church isn't here yet when the book gets opened.

Some would argue that it takes a good deal of time for this. That is what we see in the rites now approved for use in parts of Africa: much time taken to get into the rhythm of an assembly before daring to turn to God's word. That isn't likely to happen soon in many American parishes. But what few minutes of song and procession, sign of the cross and greeting, penitential rite and Gloria and opening prayer, can accomplish our entrance?

Plan changes

The Rituals of Our Entrance

What we enter is the Lord's Day assembly, the assembly that meets to do the eucharist. Though there is no single discipline to tie us all to the keeping of Sunday aside from this eucharistic assembly itself, in almost every time and place Christians have kept this day with observances that make it different from the other days. Thus people make of Sunday itself something to house their eucharist.

Think of the entrance rite as beginning in every home where parishioners live. It begins hours before, even the night before. In those hundreds of places, the baptized are making themselves ready. The ways they do this are many and depend on the makeup of the household, the working hours of adults, the distance, whether every member of the household goes or only some. But whether it is an apartment in a public housing development or a single-family house, whether there are infants or older children or only adults, whether the journey will be on foot or in a car or on public transportation, there is a procession shaping up. That is indeed the entrance procession. All the ministers eventually do is conclude it.

The entrance rite begins in baths and showers, the good human act of washing, which refreshes and prepares us. It begins in dressing. Vesture in liturgy is about color and form, festivity and attention. Some churches do it better than others. It isn't of the essence, but there can be some care for God's good creation, our bodies, and for the eyes of others. We all wear vestments, baptismal robes, when we do our liturgy.

It begins in coming hungry. At various times our church has had a preparation rite for anyone in the assembly who wished to take holy communion: fasting. An older generation remembers fasting from food and water after midnight. Now that is reduced to a symbolic hour's fast from food. This fast was never penitential but preparatory. It was about anticipation, being hungry so that understanding Christ as our food made so much sense. It may be just as well that now there is no one discipline practiced by everyone, but that does not mean there should be no discipline.

Today we need to ask how we bring to consciousness and sharpen the hunger we have for the assembly itself, for God's word in that assembly, and for the table with its thanksgiving, its bread and its wine. In some households, fasting could be counterproductive; maybe Sunday breakfast is one of the best sitting-down-together meals the household knows. In other cases, freeing oneself from food and kitchen may be freedom for reflection. But we can look beyond fasting from food. It may be that what really keeps us from knowing our hunger for the liturgy is the noise of radio and TV and idle conversation. We can fast from that.

Gathering in Our Hall

The convergence at the entryway of the building that bears our name—church—isn't quite like any other. Baptism, not blood or a common interest in sports or theater, has brought us here. Once we are here, we make no distinctions among persons. What binds us is stronger than age, sex, education, politics, wealth, common interests. Here there is no stranger, no first and no last.

Inside, the work of preparation by the sacristan and others should be completed well ahead of time. Ministers check in, ushers make a special effort to greet people, to welcome strangers, to assist any who need help. The room begins to fill. With the help of habit and ushers, it fills from the front to back and from the center of rows to their edges.

Furniture matters. How can it be at the service of the liturgy and not an obstruction? The whole space is space for liturgy, but furniture can say something quite different—and people will believe the furniture. Furniture can say: *This* place is for the audience; *that* place "up front" is where the liturgy is really done. Somehow sacristans and artists must overcome that message and use the whole room as a whole room. The routes that processions take can help in this way immensely, if they are not always simply the shortest way to get from point A to point B.

The transition is gradual. The choir might move from practicing to singing quietly behind the gathering noises. Perhaps the cantor works with those who come early on something they will be singing. We build toward the liturgy. We don't need a sharp line.

The Various Entrance Rites

If this great procession is to do its work, then its last moments must not be about ministers and musicians taking possesion of the liturgy. The work of those who prepare the liturgy is to understand the flow of the rite, the skills needed by the ministers, the particular possibilities of the liturgical seasons. A parish needs to develop the seasonal variations on this entrance and then stick with them as the seasons return year after year.

The great procession of the assembly from homes to hall concludes with what we normally call "the entrance procession." The procession of ministers becomes just the final movement of the procession we all made in arriving here. Some rooms, some seasons, may dictate dropping the procession of ministers and letting them take their places as all other members of the assembly do. Some gathering spaces are large enough for everyone to gather and go together to the place for the liturgy of the word. And some rooms cry out for processions that include choir and children, and that move down all the aisles, embracing the whole assembly.

If the procession made up of acolytes, cross bearer, lectors and presider remains the norm, then when and how it moves is important. Do those in procession act as if they are part of the assembly or somehow outside it? Do they sing? If a book is needed for the song, do those who carry neither cross nor candle nor book of the gospels hold a hymn book, and do the others join in on the chorus or refrain? Do they get the pace and know how to walk with dignity? Do their movements distract us or build us up in seeing their reverence and participation?

The Ordinary Sunday Procession

Make a list here, top to bottom, indicating first to last, of who is usually in the Sunday entrance procession.

Make a list here of a renewed entrance procession for an ordinary Sunday Mass.

_____ _____

_____ _____

_____ _____

_____ _____

_____ _____

_____ _____

_____ _____

_____ _____

_____ _____

_____ _____

_____ _____

_____ _____

Who will inform and rehearse

the ushers? _____

the servers? _____

the readers? _____

the deacons? _____

the presiders? _____

What is the time line?

The assembly sings its way into the liturgy. This is not a song to "cover" the procession time, to get ministers from "out" to "in." The entrance song takes us all in and so has to be one we can sing. It has to move us as assembly toward God's word. Its words have to bear the weight of concluding this great procession. Those who know music and those who can tell good words from poor words need a voice in this decision. Not all music published for liturgy is good for liturgy. Often a book is not needed at all, as with the litany of the saints during November. The song lasts as long as it is, as long as it is needed to do its work of giving these people a single voice. The procession of ministers happens during the song, without hurry, but the song begins before the procession and goes on even after ministers are in place.

The bow that the presider and others make before the altar is deep and without haste, a model for others. The presider then kisses the altar in such a way that this sign of familiarity and love is done on behalf of all. In this gesture, as later when the reader of the gospel kisses its pages, there is one of the identifying moments for us Catholics: people who know the holiness of a kiss. If the presider has needed a hymn book to sing in the procession, he gives it to an acolyte as he approaches the table so that both hands are free (and are placed on the table) and the whole body given to this kiss.

At the chair, the presider takes back the hymnal and continues to sing the entrance song. He hands the book to the acolyte when the song ends. The first spoken words are always "In the name of the Father, and of the Son and of the Holy Spirit." They are not rushed; they are not a greeting but a call to worship, and they accompany the reverent and full gesture known to all Catholics.

The next words are a greeting, and so are spoken to the assembly, whose response is spoken to the presider. It helps to develop a sense for these different ways in which ritual language is used. The body's orientation and the presider's gaze are shaped by the nature of any particular moment and its language. Those who believe that the only options are informal, overly dramatic or bored have never experienced the energy and passion that can be present in even the most familiar ritual expressions—whether spoken by presider or assembly. We are engaged in acclamation and dialogue here. It is not new each week, and that is exactly where its strength can come from.

The greeting may be followed by brief, invitational words to the assembly, usually but not necessarily spoken by the presider. Grasping the nature of these words has been difficult. To "briefly introduce the faithful to the Mass of the day," as the *General Instruction of the Roman Missal* states, sounds like a summary of the texts about to be heard, and that can easily become a summary of the homily. But there is another way to understand it as a strong and well-prepared summons or exhortation to take up one's responsibility for word and eucharist as this assembled church on this Lord's Day. It might echo an image from the song just sung and anticipate other images from the scriptures. Because the content and tone of these words seem to elude so many presiders, others involved in liturgy preparation can help. Let the presider know what is stronger and what is weaker. Most can learn to do better.

The penitential rite and the "Lord, have mercy," the sprinkling rite and the Gloria are all seasonal elements and will be more so in the revised sacramentary. Any one of them will give some pace to the entrance rite, slow it down a bit if done properly, which usually means that it is chanted or sung. Depending on the form of the penitential rite and "Lord, have mercy," these may be back and forth between cantor and assembly. The blessing and sprinkling of water is with sung acclamation and refrain. The Gloria is an ancient song; every assembly needs at least one if not two (ordinary and more festive) ways of singing it.

In practice, a parish comes to have a way of entering the liturgy that is peculiar to each season. This is so because the entrance rite must prepare the assembly to participate in the liturgy of this day, this particular day. The Sundays of Easter differ from the Sundays of Lent. This is embodied in the choice of entrance processional song and in the ordering of the other rites before the opening prayer. Thus Christmas days emphasize the Gloria, lenten Sundays the penitential rite; all the Sundays of Easter season have an exuberant sprinkling rite. Likewise, within each season, the entrance processional song may carry from one week to another, sometimes with different verses, but always giving the "sound" to the season.

The effort here is not simply toward one Advent or one Lent but toward a parish practice for Advent or Lent that can be claimed year after year. It will evolve, but it need not be reinvented year after year.

Let Us Pray

Invariably the entrance rite concludes with the summons to pray, silence and the opening prayer proclaimed by the presider. All three elements are important. First comes the summons to pray: This is more a command than a tentative invitation. Then comes the silence: The acolyte already has the book in place and the presider keeps the silence and stillness long enough for all to settle into it. The silent time should be consistent: Mass to Mass, presider to presider, week to week, season to season. It will take time for it to get into the rhythm of each body and the body as a whole, but it will happen.

Finally, the prayer is spoken or chanted. Like the readings, it takes preparation. There is hope that the new sacramentary will offer both stronger translations of the Latin texts and original texts for each Sunday. These latter take their inspiration from the readings of the day.

The invitation and the prayer itself may be chanted. At its best, this both lifts the prayer up to be a fitting conclusion to

The Gloria

What settings of the Gloria does the parish know well? Which settings are more "ordinary" and which are more "festive"? (Mark each with an O or an F.)

_____ _____

_____ _____

_____ _____

_____ _____

_____ _____

_____ _____

_____ _____

_____ _____

_____ _____

_____ _____

_____ _____

Do we need to learn another setting? _____

Do we need a Gloria in another language? _____

List any settings that come to mind below.

_____

_____

_____

the entrance rites and assures that its words are heard well by the assembly. But chanted or spoken, the prayer needs preparation so that it is not in one ear and out the other after a quick Amen. Here are words of prayer particular to this day's liturgy alone. They should have entered into the homilist's thought and the presider's preparation for the liturgy. A presider's time and energy must go into becoming familiar with these words and with the way to pray them aloud.

An assembly can say Amen to such a prayer and sense that the time of preparation is ended. This Amen is the Amen of an assembly, formed by our procession and song, silence and prayer, and ready now for listening to God's word as the church here assembled.

The Rituals of Our Dispersal

When all have said Amen to the prayer after communion, only the blessing and dismissal remain, but provision is made in the *General Instruction of the Roman Missal* (#123) for announcements before the blessing.

The willingness of people to hear announcements, parish doings that may take a while to tell about, is related not to whether some imagined time limit (an hour?) has now been violated but to whether week-in and week-out the liturgy just celebrated is fully theirs to participate in.

By all means, the bulletin should be well done and inviting, and should contain important details and phone numbers. But the vitality of a parish is grasped even more in this announcement time at the end of Mass. These are not small matters but the life of the parish, events and needs that all should know about. Here, the communal, the social, the catechetical, the sacramental and the justice dimensions of parish life are all to be heard.

Most announcements are not best made by the presider. It is better if one parishioner after another comes to the cantor's microphone or another place (not the ambo, though) to speak briefly. Thus people can put a face on an event or a need. Over time, even those on the fringes of parish life acquire some sense for the diversity of works and people, and may become willing to be more involved. The assembly and presider and other ministers remain seated. Someone (an usher?) oversees this so that written announcements that have no spokesperson at a particular Mass can still be made. The last announcement is always the recessional hymn made by the cantor. (If no books are needed for this or if it is apparent by the layout of the song sheet, then no announcement needs to be made.)

Then the presider stands and all stand. The presider gives the blessing in the long or short form, and the dismissal immediately follows. Both blessing and dismissal, with their responses, may be chanted, but only if this can be done consistently. When there is a deacon, it is the deacon's role to give the dismissal.

The recessional, though not explicitly called for in the *General Instruction,* has taken hold in most parishes as a way to bring a good conclusion to time together. Some seasons may best end in quiet, but the "closing hymn" will be the norm. Presider and other ministers may stay in place for a verse or two, singing, then form the procession and make their way through the assembly, still singing. A wide variety of music may be good for this recessional. The sense of the season should echo in both sound and words in the hearts of all those who now leave to love and serve the Lord. A wide variety of music may be good for this recessional. This is the place where the parish repertoire may grow to include strong, lively compositions from various traditions (for example, "Soon and very soon" during November or Advent, "We are marching in the light of God" or "Resucitó" during Eastertime).

The Ministries

Train the ministers

Presider, cantor and other musicians, acolytes and ushers are the primary ministers in these rites. So is the sacristan. Meeting in their own groups, they can read and discuss their experiences and work together on goals. But as the parish refines an overall approach to the entrance and dismissal rites, or as the parish moves toward a distinctive rite for Advent or Eastertime, all these ministers could come together to learn about it and, especially, to practice.

Most of what is needed for catechesis with individual ministries is provided in the resources listed above. Ushers, who are crucial to both entrance and dismissal, can study and discuss their role using *Guide for Ushers.* Acolytes will find help in *Serve God with Gladness.*

The sacristan, whose role is essential if the presider is to be free to focus on the assembly, should check well before the starting time to be certain that every book and vessel and other object is in place. Near the beginning, the sacristan should put the procession in order, see that vesture is worn properly and objects carried properly. It may also be the sacristan's responsibility to see that the procession doesn't bunch up but spreads itself out.

The cantor and other musicians should work to understand how these rites of entrance and exit are sung. If the assembly can begin the liturgy with their song, they will be ready to sing the Gloria, the psalm, and so on. The initial song as much as any other element of the entrance rite confirms in all the sense that here is a church, not so many individuals, but a community that is lifting up its single song to the Lord. And if the assembly can conclude the liturgy with their song, they will take it back to homes and neighborhoods. The singing that begins and ends the liturgy will little by little nourish the common sense that liturgy is something sung.

In these processional pieces musicians should find opportunities for creative back-and-forth singing between assembly and choir, for use of instruments, or for great simplicity.

Respect for repetition within a season or a segment of Ordinary Time means building a repertoire of music that is worthy of repetition. More than any other music of the liturgy these pieces that begin and end are going to give a sound and content to the seasons as they come year after year.

When the parish has worked toward a liturgy that is sung, the cantor will have responsibility for leading the assembly in some element of the entrance rite: penitential rite and Kyrie, sprinkling rite, and/or Gloria. Here, as in the responsorial psalm, the gospel acclamation and, if sung, the intercessions, the cantor is a leader of the assembly's prayer and not simply a leader of their song. In fact, the assembly's song will hardly need leading as time goes by, but the cantor's role does not diminish at all.

Finally, many presiders need the help of critical observers to find the best way to process, bow, kiss the altar, lead the sign of the cross and greeting, speak briefly, and lead the opening prayer. Presiders here and in other parts of the liturgy need to know when the voice should be amplified (for example, the sign of the cross) and when it is not (for example, the Gloria, or any other time that the presider is simply joining the assembly in reciting or singing the assembly's words).

These rites are not about how friendly we can be with one another. The presider who engages in this kind of banter takes liturgy away from the assembly and makes it something that this presider does and the rest of us are supposed to enjoy. Adding friendly greetings, even before the sign of the cross, using one's own words instead of the scriptural greetings after the sign of the cross, telling the assembly to be seated after the Amen of the opening prayer, is disrespectful to the liturgy and to the assembly.

On the other extreme is the presider who acts as if liturgy is a machine that runs by itself as long as all is done in the right order. Careless, absent presiding may use the right words and the right gestures, but it denies all the energy of the liturgy.

It is crucial that those responsible for the ministries come to know their craft here, to know how to fashion and hold to parish entrance rites, in which the church comes to know well and care greatly about the beauty that they create in these moments. A parish should strive for a basic entrance rite (and for wide variations on it to make entrance to the seasons) that is a whole, worthy of being done again and again because it is so involving, because it works so well at taking the assembly into the liturgy. Two parishes can have that same order of entrance on paper, but it will be an entrance in one place and a distraction in another. The difference is in the attitude and skills of ministers.

Catechesis for the Assembly

Catechize the assembly

This, then, is the year that the whole assembly, all ministers included, should receive some catechesis about our rites of entering and leave-taking. By now the parish should know well how to use various forums for this, especially the bulletin and existing groups. The Sunday homily will be basic, and it should be interesting to choose three or four Sundays in the course of the year when such preaching will be most appropriate. As in other years, this is mystagogy, wherein preacher and assembly ponder common experiences and take on the challenge of a fully participatory liturgy Sunday after Sunday. As in other years, all who do catechesis with children, youth and adults should be invited to enter into this discussion and plan ways in which they also will catechize about these entrance rites.

It's All of Us Entering

Much has been said on this above. It needs to be explored with the assembly. We are the church, and when the book is opened for the first reading of scripture, we should have gotten ourselves together and be ready to listen. Explore how this begins: Everyone has the responsibility to prepare for Sunday liturgy and this can take many forms, but some elements are worth striving for in every household (for example, looking at the scriptures and even talking about them beforehand, some sort of "fasting" to come hungry for the assembly and God's word and the eucharist).

There may be occasion here to discuss the whole context of the Lord's Day using the letter of John Paul II *Dies Domini* (available from LTP as *Guide to Keeping Sunday Holy*). Discussing the whole of the Lord's Day, and all that can make that difficult for today's households, is the only way to explore realistically (and here a homilist needs to be in dialogue with these households) how Sunday Mass can be more than just another item on the Sunday agenda.

This is the time to discuss the important ministry of ushers in the parish and how they need cooperation in helping us fill the room beginning with the places nearest the altar and working back, and always moving into the pews or benches, not clinging to the aisles.

How important is coming on time? The assembly needs to know two things: First, there's a responsibility, a duty we're told, to this participation, and that means being on hand for all of it. Second, it is inevitable that some will be late, and the presumption must always be it couldn't be helped. The etiquette of the latecomers also needs discussion, especially if there is no practice of waiting to seat people until the gospel acclamation.

How important is being here until we're all ready to leave? This usually takes care of itself as a parish works on its liturgy, but people need to know: Everyone needs you! If you have to leave on occasion, we presume there's good reason. But know this: The Mass doesn't take an hour. It doesn't take 55 minutes or 65 minutes. It takes what it takes for us all to do these holy deeds well.

Is it true that some of us are here because we "have to be," because the church has a law? Talk about the obligation to Sunday liturgy, but see it as that "duty" spoken of in article 14 of the *Constitution on the Sacred Liturgy.* As the baptized, we are obliged to be here, to constitute the church and to take part fully, consciously, actively. We are needed; that is why we are obliged.

Out of whatever preaching is done, the image the whole parish might carry is that the entrance procession begins hours before Mass in all the bedrooms and kitchens of the assembly, slowly shapes up and gathers momentum as people come on foot and by vehicle and start to fill this room of ours until, last of all or nearly so, the presider and other ministers take their places within the assembly, and the church is at last ready to hear the word of the Lord, to give God thanks and praise, and to share in holy communion.

At Home and in the Assembly

Insights for the homilist or catechist into some elements of these rites are found in *Preaching about the Mass* and *Saving Signs, Wondrous Words.* In these matters connections can be made between ritual in the assembly and ritual in households. The sign of the cross we make on our bodies all together on Sunday is not the only time in a week when we make that gesture. How does it mark our mornings and nights and meal prayers? And what does it mean for us? And what are the various gestures with which we make the cross on our bodies? Mystagogical preaching should draw on what we proclaim about the cross on Good Friday and in the Sunday eucharistic prayer, and should ponder what it is to associate this to our bodies again and again through our lives.

Likewise, the penitential rite done by the assembly on Sunday echoes some element of a Catholic's daily prayer at night, at bedtime perhaps, asking God's mercy for the day's wrongs and proclaiming how we are saved by that mercy.

Even the seemingly small deed of kissing the altar can be reflected on within a homily. Not only is the altar kissed but the book as well (after the gospel is proclaimed), and our peace greeting is often called "the kiss of peace." On Good Friday, the cross is kissed. Catholics of the Byzantine tradition kiss icons. What is this simple gesture, and does it have a place in our lives? Because the blessing and sprinkling of water will likely be part of the entrance rite, at least in the Easter season, the place of water in Catholic life can also be part of this catechesis at the appropriate time.

We come to the deeds of Sunday out of the deeds we have rehearsed all week. So it is with song. What can our song be if this one hour a week is all the song we have? Where in the home are refrains and acclamations, perhaps as part of table prayer? At a time when music is so plentiful but when we ourselves sing so little, catechesis reflects on how we as Christians must not deprive ourselves of our songs, for in song is our faith made firm, and in song God is praised and the tradition is handed on to another generation.

Implement the changes

List the particular changes you will undertake.	Beginning date	Check-up date

Now What Do We Do?

Now that you have worked through this five-year or five-phase process, what other matters liturgical need to be addressed? Use the following pages to keep a running list of brainstormed ideas, details that need attention, or long-range projects that may have arisen out of the last five years' worth of work.

Implement the changes

Implement the changes

Implement the changes

Implement the changes

Implement the changes

Implement the changes

Implement the changes

Implement the changes

Implement the changes